Janice VanCleave's
Astronomy for Every Kid

The Janice VanCleave

SCIENCE FOR EVERY KID

Series

Janice VanCleave's
Astronomy for Every Kid
101 Easy Experiments that Really Work

Janice Pratt VanCleave

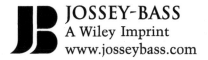

JOSSEY-BASS
A Wiley Imprint
www.josseybass.com

Dedicated to one of my best friends,
Patsy Ruth Ross Henderson

Illustrated by Barbara Clark.

Published by Jossey-Bass
A Wiley Imprint
989 Market Street, San Francisco, CA 94103-1741   www.josseybass.com

Published simultaneously in Canada.

The publisher and the author have made every reasonable effort to ensure that the experiments and activities in this book are safe when conducted as instructed but assume no responsibility for any damage caused or sustained while performing the experiments or activities in *Janice VanCleave's Astronomy for Every Kid*. Parents, guardians, and/or teachers should supervise young readers who undertake the experiments and activities in this book.

Readers should be aware that Internet Web sites offered as citations and/or sources for further information may have changed or disappeared between the time this was written and when it is read.

Jossey-Bass books and products are available through most bookstores. To contact Jossey-Bass directly call our Customer Care Department within the U.S. at 800-956-7739, outside the U.S. at 317-572-3986, or fax 317-572-4002.

Jossey-Bass also publishes its books in a variety of electronic formats. Some content that appears in print may not be available in electronic books.

Library of Congress Cataloging-in-Publication Data

VanCleave, Janice Pratt.
    [Astronomy for every kid]
    Janice VanCleave's astronomy for every kid : 101 easy experiments that really work / Janice Pratt VanCleave.
        p.   cm. — (Wiley science editions)
    Includes bibliographical references.
    Summary: An elementary science experiment book that provides young scientists with safe, workable astronomy projects.
    ISBN 0-471-54285-7 (lib. bdg.). — ISBN 0-471-53573-7 (paper)
    1. Astronomy—Experiments—Juvenile literature. [1. Astronomy
—Experiments. 2. Experiments.] I. Title. II. Series.
QB46.V38   1991
520—dc20   91-2443

FIRST EDITION
PB Printing   20 19 18 17 16

Preface

This is an elementary science experiment book and like its predecessors *Biology for Every Kid, Chemistry for Every Kid, Earth Science for Every Kid,* and *Physics for Every Kid,* it is designed to teach that SCIENCE IS FUN. Astronomy is more than stories about the constellations, the order of the planets and how many moons or rings they might have. It is a study of how your life is affected by the things on and beyond the earth's atmosphere as well as how celestial bodies affect each other. The 101 astronomy experiments are designed for children ages 8 to 12. Young children will be able to successfully complete the experiments with adult supervision. Older children can easily follow the step-by-step instructions and complete the experiments with little or no adult help. Special warnings are given when adult assistance might be required.

The book contains 101 experiments relating to astronomy. Each experiment has a purpose, list of materials, step-by-step instructions and illustrations, expected results, and a scientific explanation in understandable terms.

The introductory purpose for each experiment gives the reader a clue to the concept that will be introduced. The purpose is complete enough to present the goal, but does not give away the mystery of the results.

Materials are needed, but in all the experiments the necessary items are easily obtained. Most of the materials are readily available around the house. A list of the necessary supplies is given for each experiment.

Detailed step-by-step instructions are given along with illustrations. Pretesting of all the activities preceded the drafting of the instructions. The experiments are SAFE and they WORK.

Expected results are described to direct the experimenter further. They provide immediate positive reinforcement to the student who has performed the experiment properly, and they help correct the student who doesn't achieve the desired results.

Another special feature of the book is the Why? section, which gives a scientific explanation for each result in terms that are easily understood.

This book was written to provide young scientists with safe, workable astronomy experiments. The objective of the book is to make the learning of what happens in the universe a rewarding experience and, thus encourage a student's desire to seek more knowledge about science.

Note:

The experiments and activities in this book should be performed with care and according to the instructions provided. Any person conducting a scientific experiment should read the instructions before beginning the experiment. An adult should supervise young readers who undertake the experiments and activities featured in this book. The publisher accepts no responsibility for any damage caused or sustained while performing the experiments or activities covered by this book.

Contents

Introduction

Astronomy is the study of celestial bodies. This science includes information about the planet we live on—Earth—and all our neighbors in space. Studying astronomy, like all sciences, is a way of solving problems and discovering why things happen the way they do. Since ancient times, humans have been interested in the world around them. Shepherds spent their evenings viewing the ever-changing drama in the sky. The stories about the imaginary figures in the heavens are still being told and enjoyed today. Some of the earliest known astronomers were the Egyptians. About 5000 B.C., the Egyptians believed their valley—the Nile Valley—to be the lower boundary for the entire universe. The mountains surrounding the land were thought to be holding up the sky with its fixed stars that could be touched if one could climb to the top of one of the mountains. The sun god rode across the sky on a large barge each day and returned behind the mountains each night. These early astronomers were forming the best conclusions from the facts available to them. As time passed, each generation gathered new information, and new knowledge about the universe continually corrected the false ideas of fixed stars and riding sun gods. Man has not climbed high enough to touch the stars yet, but new technology has allowed him to leave his footprints on his closest neighbor, the moon. Much information has been gathered about celestial bodies, but we have barely scratched the surface of the knowledge yet to be uncovered. This book has no new facts to offer, but it will provide fun experiments that teach known astronomy concepts.

This book will help you to make the most of the exciting scientific era in which we live. It will guide you in discovering answers to questions such as: What is a barycenter? Why is the resolution of the Hubble telescope so high? Why is Venus so hot? When is Neptune the outer planet? What is a nebula? How is a black hole formed? The answers to these questions and many more will be discovered by performing the fun, safe, and workable experiments in this book.

The reader will be rewarded with successful results if he or she reads an experiment carefully, follows each step in order, and does not substitute equipment. It is suggested that the experiments within a group be performed in order. There is some build up of information from the first to the last, but any terms defined in a previous experiment can be found in the Glossary. Terms defined in the Glossary appear in italic. Two goals of this book are to guide you through the steps necessary to successfully complete a science experiment and to teach the best method of solving problems and discovering answers. The following is the standard pattern for each experiment in the book:

1. Purpose: A statement of the basic goals for the experiment.
2. Materials: A list of necessary supplies.
3. Procedure: Step-by-step instructions on how to perform the experiment.
4. Results: An explanation exactly stating what is expected to happen. This is an immediate learning tool. If

2

the expected results are achieved, the experimenter has an immediate positive reinforcement. A "foul-up" is also quickly recognized, and the need to start over or make corrections is readily apparent.

5. Why? An explanation of why the results were achieved, described in terms that are understandable to the reader who may not be familiar with scientific terms.

General Instructions for the Reader

1. **Read first.** Read each experiment completely before starting.
2. **Collect needed supplies.** Less frustration and more fun will be experienced if all the necessary materials for the experiments are ready for instant use. You lose your train of thought when you have to stop and search for supplies.
3. **Experiment.** Do not rush into the experiment. Follow each step very carefully, never skip steps, and do not add your own. Safety is of utmost importance, and by reading any experiment before starting, then following the instructions exactly, you can feel confident that no unexpected results will occur.
4. **Observe.** If your results are not the same as described in the experiment, carefully reread the instructions, and start over from step one.

Measurement Substitutions

Measuring quantities described in this book are intended to be those commonly used in every kitchen. When specific amounts are given, you need to use a measuring instrument closest to the described amount. The quantities listed are not critical and a variation of very small amounts more or less will not alter the results.

English to SI Substitutions

English	SI (Metric)

LIQUID MEASUREMENTS

English	SI (Metric)
1 gallon	4 liters
1 quart	1 liter
1 pint	500 milliliters
1 cup (8 oz.)	250 milliliters
1 ounce	30 milliliters
1 tablespoon	15 milliliters
1 teaspoon	5 milliliters

LENGTH MEASUREMENTS

English	SI (Metric)
1 yard	1 meter
1 foot (12 inches)	1/3 meter
1 inch	2.54 centimeters
1 mile	1.61 kilometers

PRESSURE

English	SI (Metric)
14.7 pounds per square inch (PSI)	1 atmosphere

Abbreviations

atmosphere = atm
centimeter = cm
cup = c
gallon = gal.
pint = pt.
quart = qt.
ounce = oz.
tablespoon = T.
teaspoon = tsp.

liter = l
milliliter = ml
meter = m
millimeter = mm
kilometer = km
yard = yd.
foot = ft.
inch = in.

4

I
Planets

1. Cooler

Purpose To determine how color affects a planet's surface temperature.

Materials *2 thermometers*
desk lamp
ruler
construction paper, 1 piece white and 1 piece black
scissors
cellophane tape
2 empty metal food cans, same size
Caution: Be sure rims are not jagged. They might cut your hands.

Procedure
- *Cut a piece of white and of black construction paper to fit around the outside of the cans, much as the can label does.*
- *Secure one piece of paper to each can with tape.*
- *Place one thermometer inside each can.*
- *Read and record the temperature on both thermometers.*
- *Position both cans about 12 in. (30 cm) from the lamp.*
- *Turn the lamp on.*
- *Read and record the temperature on both thermometers after 10 minutes.*

Results The temperature is much higher in the can covered with black paper.

Why? The dark paper absorbs more light waves than does the white paper. The white paper is cooler because it reflects more of the light waves than does the black paper. The absorption of the light waves increases the temperature of a material. The lighter the surface material on a planet, the less light energy the planet's surface absorbs and the cooler is its surface.

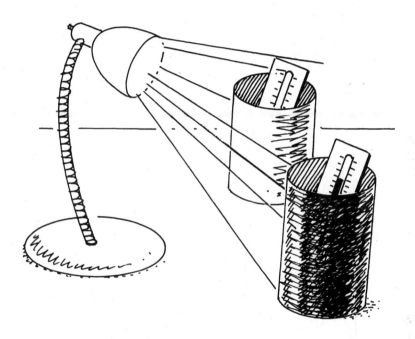

2. Shaded

Purpose To demonstrate how a planet's surface temperature can vary.

Materials *2 thermometers*

Procedure

- *Read and record the temperature on both thermometers.*
- *Place one thermometer on the ground in the shade of a tree or other large structure.*
- *Place the second thermometer on the ground, but in the direct light of the Sun.*
  Note: It is important that both thermometers be placed on the same type of surface (grass works well).
- *Read and record the temperature on both thermometers after 20 minutes.*

Results The temperature of the surface in the shade is lower than the same surface in direct sunlight.

Why? The tree or large structure blocks some of the light rays, producing a shaded area on the ground. This protected surface area is cooler due to the decrease in light energy received. The same type of surface in direct sunlight receives more light energy and becomes hotter. The temperature of the surface of planets can vary depending on the landscape. If there are large structures to provide shade, the temperature of the shaded surface will be cooler.

HOTTER TEMPERATURE

9

3. Bent

Purpose To demonstrate how the thickness of an atmosphere affects the bending of light.

Materials *2 drinking cups*
2 shiny pennies
modeling clay, 2 grape-sized pieces

Procedure

- *Stick the pieces of clay in the inside bottom of each cup.*
- *Press a penny in the clay so that it is in the very center of the cup. Do this in both cups.*
- *Fill one cup with water.*
- *Place both cups on the edge of a table. The cups must be side by side and even with the edge of the table.*
- *Stand close to the table.*
- *Take some steps backward while observing the pennies in the cups.*
- *Stop when you can no longer see the pennies in either cup.*

Results The penny in the cup filled with air disappears from view first, while you can still see the penny in the cup filled with water.

Why? You see the penny in the water at a greater distance because light enters the cup, reflects from the penny, hits the surface of the water, and is bent at an angle (*refracted*) toward your eye. The water is thicker than the air and thicker materials refract the light more. A change in the thickness of the Earth's atmosphere due to pollution increases the refraction of light. Venus' thick atmosphere refracts light much more than does the Earth's atmosphere. An observer on Venus would see many mirages and distortions because of this.

CUP WITH WATER IN IT

4. Too Close

Purpose To determine how distance from the Sun affects atmospheric temperature.

Materials 2 thermometers
1 desk lamp
yardstick (meter stick)

Procedure

■ *Place one thermometer on the 4 in. (10 cm) mark and the second thermometer on the 36 in. (100 cm) mark of the ruler.*
■ *Position the lamp at the 0 end of the ruler.*
■ *Turn the lamp on.*
■ *Read and record the temperatures on both thermometers after 10 minutes.*

Results The temperature is hotter on the closer thermometer.

Why? The thermometer closer to the lamp receives more energy and thus gets hotter. As the light moves away from the lamp, rays leaving at an angle do not hit the distant thermometer. The atmosphere of a planet is heated in a similar way. Mercury is the planet closest to the Sun and receives the most energy. Planets farther from the Sun receive less heat and have cooler atmospheres. Mercury is much hotter than Pluto, which is very far from the Sun. Other factors such as density and pressure also affect the atmospheric temperature. These factors are discussed in later experiments.

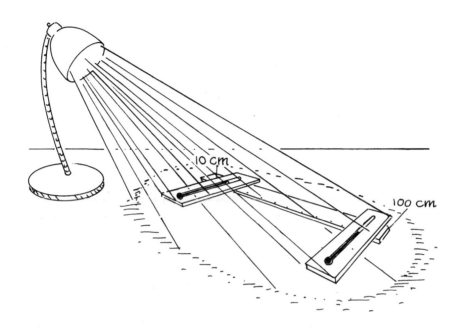

10 cm

100 cm

light

13

5. Quicker

Purpose To determine how distance affects a planet's period of revolution.

Materials *yardstick (meter stick)*
ruler
modeling clay

Procedure

- *Place a walnut-sized ball of clay on one end of the ruler and on one end of the yardstick (meter stick).*
- *Hold the yardstick and ruler vertically, side by side, with the edge without the clay ball on the ground.*
- *Release both at the same time.*

Results The shorter ruler hits the surface first.

Why? The clay ball on the yardstick has farther to fall than does the ball on the shorter ruler. This is similar to the movement of the planets, which are continuously "falling" around the Sun. Mercury, with the shortest distance from the Sun, 36 million miles (57.96 million km), takes only 88 Earth days to make its voyage around the Sun. Pluto has a much longer path to follow—it is 3,688 million miles (5,900 million km) away from the Sun and requires 248 Earth years to complete its period of revolution (time to move around the Sun).

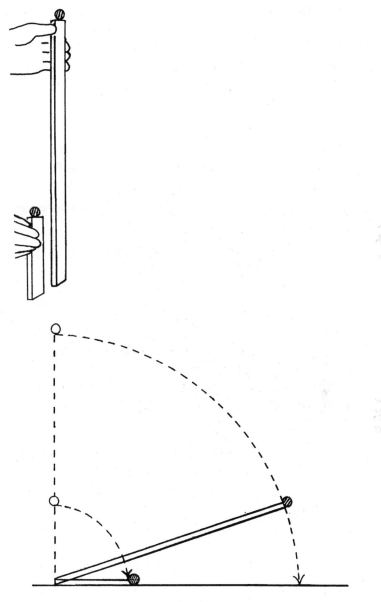

6. Hidden

Purpose To demonstrate how Mercury's position affects the observation of its surface.

Materials *desk lamp*
pencil

Procedure
- *Turn the lamp on with the glowing bulb facing you.*
  Caution: Do not look directly into the lamp.
- *Grasp the pencil in the center with the print on the pencil facing you.*
- *Hold the pencil at arm's length from your face and about 6 in. (15 cm) from the glowing bulb.*

Results The print cannot be read on the pencil, and the color of the pencil is difficult to determine.

Why? The light behind the pencil is so bright that it is difficult to see the surface of the pencil. In a similar way, the glare of the Sun behind the planet Mercury makes it difficult to study the planet's surface. Mercury is less than half the size of the Earth and the closest planet to the Sun. From the Earth, astronomers are looking almost directly into the Sun when they view Mercury. The first photographs of one-third of the planet's surface were taken in 1974 and 1975 when the Mariner 10 space probe flew about 200 miles (320 km) from the surface of Mercury.

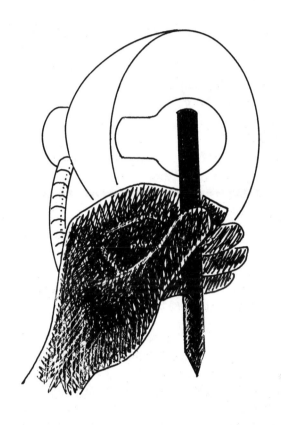

17

7. Cover Up

Purpose To determine why Mercury does not cause an eclipse.

Materials *desk lamp*
your thumb

Procedure

- *Stand about 2 yd. (2 m) from the desk lamp.*
- *Close your right eye.*
- *Hold your left thumb at arm's length in front of your left eye and in front of the lamp.*
- *Slowly move your thumb toward your face until it is directly in front of your open eye.*

Results The farther your thumb is from your eye, the smaller your thumb appears and the more of the lamp you see.

Why? Your thumb blocked the light moving from the lamp toward your eye. The closer your thumb is to your face, the more light it blocks. Because Mercury is very close to the Sun, it blocks only a small portion of the Sun's light, as did your thumb when held close to the lamp. The shadow made by Mercury's position between the Earth and the Sun is a very small dot. The shadow made by Mercury is so small that it does not spread out enough to fall on the Earth, but lands in space. For this reason, Mercury does not cause a *solar eclipse*.

18

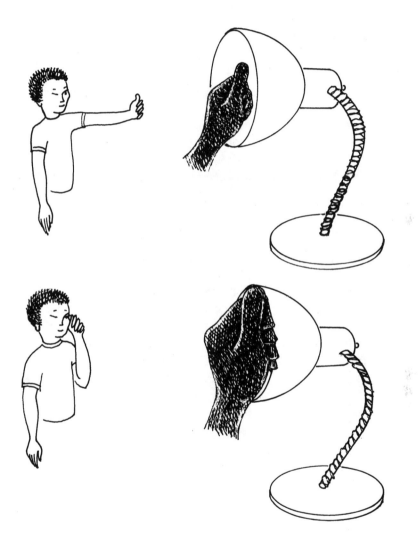

8. Thick

Purpose To determine why Venus' atmosphere is so hard to see through.

Materials *flashlight*
wax paper

Procedure
- *Turn the flashlight on and place it on the edge of a table.*
- *Stand about 2 yd. (2 m) from the table.*
- *Face the light and observe its brightness.*
- *Hold a sheet of wax paper in front of your face.*
- *Look through the wax paper at the light.*

Results The light looks blurred through the paper.

Why? The light rays bounce off the wax paper. This is similar to the way light bounces off carbon dioxide molecules in the atmosphere above Venus. There are 100,000 times as many carbon dioxide molecules in Venus' atmosphere as in the Earth's atmosphere. Even though the carbon dioxide gas is colorless, it is difficult to observe the surface of Venus because the light rays bounce around, producing blurred images.

9. Hot Box

Purpose To determine why Venus is so hot.

Materials 2 thermometers
1 jar tall enough to hold one of the
thermometers
1 lid for the jar

Procedure

- *Put one thermometer inside the jar and close the lid.*
- *Place the second thermometer and the jar near a window in direct sunlight.*
- *Record the temperature on both thermometers after 20 minutes.*

Results The temperature inside the closed jar is higher than outside the jar.

Why? *Solar radiation* includes both visible and *infrared* light waves. *Visible* waves make up the colors seen in rainbows—red, orange, yellow, green, blue, and violet. Infrared waves are given off by hot objects. The glass jar, like the Venusian atmosphere, is nearly *opaque* to infrared waves, that is, it does not allow the waves to pass through. Much of the sunlight that reaches the surface of the planet, or bottom of the jar, is absorbed, thus heating up the planet or the jar. The hot surface then re-radiates the energy as heat (infrared). It is these infrared rays that are trapped within the jar and within the atmosphere of the planet. The atmosphere on Venus contains 100,000 times as much carbon dioxide as that found in the Earth's atmosphere. The trapped infrared waves warm the planet's surface to more than 800.6°F (427°C). At this temperature, a self-cleaning oven turns food to dust. On Venus' hot surface, rocks glow red, like coils in an electric oven.

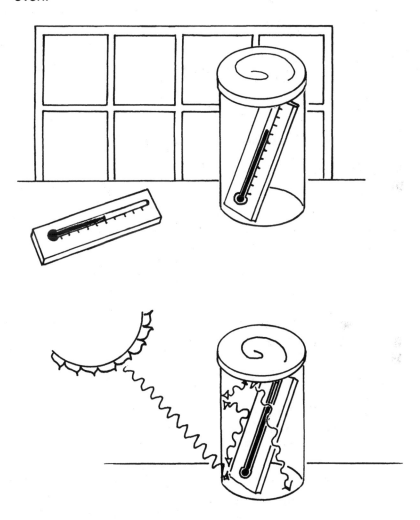

10. In Place

Purpose To demonstrate the point of balance between the Earth and its Moon.

Materials *pencil*
modeling clay
push tack
wax paper
black marker
ruler
scissors

Procedure

- *Cut a circle with about a 4 in. (10 cm) diameter from the wax paper.*
- *Stick the push tack through the center of the paper circle and into the side of the pencil's eraser.*
- *Use the marker to make a black dot on the pencil 1/2 in. (1 cm) inside the edge of the paper circle.*
- *Stick a small grape-sized piece of clay on the opposite end of the pencil.*
- *Rotate the paper circle and observe the position of the black dot.*
- *Hold the paper and rotate the pencil.*

Results The black dot always stays between the paper circle and the clay ball, and it remains about 1/2 in. (1 cm) from inside the edge of the paper.

Why? Your model uses a pencil to connect the clay Moon and paper Earth. The dot represents the *center of gravity* of this Earth-Moon system (a point at which all the weight seems to be concentrated, also referred to as the system's balancing point). This point of balance is called the *barycenter*. The Earth-Moon system revolves around the Sun like a single body. The point of rotation of this system is the barycenter and, as the model demonstrates, this is not a definite place on the Earth, but a distance of about 1,000 miles (1,600 km) within the Earth's surface on the side facing the Moon.

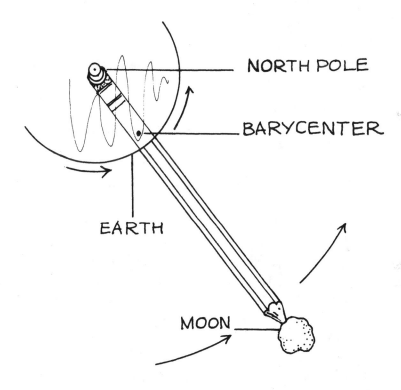

NORTH POLE

BARYCENTER

EARTH

MOON

11. Rotate

Purpose To demonstrate a method of proving that the Earth rotates.

Materials *record player*
wide-mouthed glass jar, 1 qt. (1 liter)
pencil
string
washer
scissors
masking tape, 2 in. (5 cm) wide

Procedure

- *Tie a string to the washer.*
- *Cut the string so that it is about three-quarters the height of the jar used.*
- *Tie the string to the center of the pencil.*
- *Place the pencil across the mouth of the jar so that the washer hangs in the center.*
- *Place the tape in the center of the turntable.*
- *Center the jar on top of the roll of tape.*
- *Turn the record player on to the lowest speed.*
- *Adjust the position of the jar and pencil so that the string hangs straight down as the turntable spins.*
- *Stop the turntable and tape the pencil so that it does not move.*
- *Start the washer spinning back and forth.*
- *Turn the record player on again to its lowest speed and observe the movement of the washer.*

Results The washer continues to swing back and forth in the same direction even though the glass is turning around.

Why? *Inertia* is the resistance to any change in motion. The washer keeps swinging in the same direction because of its inertia. A pendulum could be suspended at the North Pole of the Earth to prove that the Earth rotates. The pendulum would continue to swing in the same direction, while the Earth beneath it would make one complete turn in 24 hours.

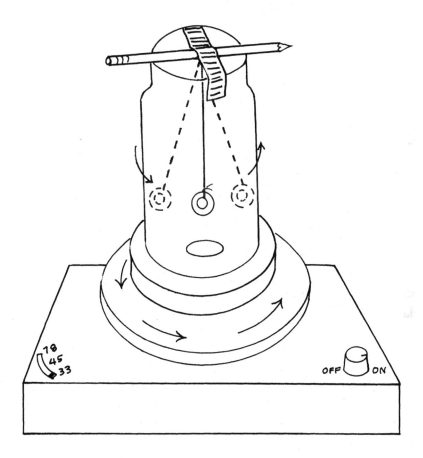

12. Blue Sky

Purpose To determine why the Earth is called the blue planet.

Materials *flashlight*
drinking glass
eye dropper
milk
spoon

Procedure

- *Fill the glass with water.*
- *In a darkened room, use the flashlight to direct a light beam through the center of the water.*
- *Add 1 drop of milk to the water and stir.*
- *Again, shine the light through the water.*

Results The light passes through the clear water, but the milky water has a pale blue-gray look.

Why? The waves of color in white light each have a different size. The particles of milk in the water separate and spread the small blue waves from the light throughout the water, causing the water to appear blue. Nitrogen and oxygen molecules in the Earth's atmosphere, like the milk particles, are small enough to separate out the small blue light waves from sunlight. The blue light spreads out through the atmosphere, making the sky look blue from the Earth and giving the entire planet a blue look when it is observed from space. The color in the glass is not a bright blue because more than just the blue light waves are being scattered by large particles in the milk. This happens in the atmosphere when large quantities of dust or water vapor scatter more than just the blue light waves. Clean, dry air produces the deepest blue sky color because the blue waves in the light are scattered the most.

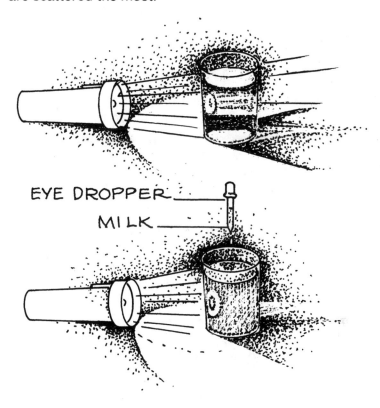

EYE DROPPER

MILK

13. Back Up

Purpose To demonstrate the apparent backward motion of Mars.

Materials *helper*

Procedure
- *This is an outside activity.*
- *Ask a helper to stand next to you and then to slowly start walking forward.*
- *Look past your helper's head and notice the background objects that he or she passes.*
- *Start walking toward your helper at a faster speed than your helper.*
- *Continue to observe the background past your helper's head.*
- *Stop and ask your helper to stop when you are about 5 yd. (5 m) in front of him or her.*

Results At first, you are looking forward to view the background past your helper, but as you take the lead you must look backward to see your helper and the objects beyond.

Why? Your helper is not going backward; you are simply looking from a different position. Mars was thought by early observers to move forward, stop, go backward, and then go forward again. Actually the planet was continuing forward on its *orbit* around the Sun while the Earth was zipping around the Sun in one-half the time of Mars' trip. Earth speeds ahead of Mars during part of the time, giving Mars the appearance of moving backwards. Mars appears

30

to move forward when the Earth races around the orbit and approaches Mars from behind. This apparent change in the direction of Mars is called *retrograde* motion.

14. Sun Prints

Purpose To determine what might cause Jupiter's colored clouds.

Materials *double-sided tape*
photographic paper (This can be purchased at a photography store, or ask your local newspaper or high school photography club for a sheet of outdated developing paper. Keep it out of the sunlight.)
cardboard
scissors

Procedure

■ *Cut a heart design from the cardboard.*

■ *In a semidarkened room, use the double-sided tape to stick the heart to the glossy side of the developing paper.*

■ *Take the paper outside and allow the Sun to shine directly on the paper for one minute.*

■ *Return to the darkened room and take the paper heart off the developing paper.*

Results The developing paper is unchanged under the cardboard. A light-colored, heart-shaped design is surrounded by a dark background.

Why? The developing paper turns dark when light hits it because the light chemically activates the molecules on the glossy surface of the paper. The darkness of the paper depends on how much light it receives. The cardboard did not allow light to pass through, so the paper under the cardboard remained the same color. This effect of the Sun on the photographic paper may be the answer to the mysteriously swirling sea of colored clouds in Jupiter's atmosphere. Part of the mystery of the clouds is that the colors stay separated and do not blend together. Jupiter's atmosphere is made mostly of hydrogen and helium—two colorless gases. Scientists think that the colors may come from chemicals in the clouds that change color because of Jupiter's lightning or that the Sun changes the colors as it did the special light-sensitive photographic paper.

SUN

15. Red Spot

Purpose To demonstrate the movement in Jupiter's red spot.

Materials *wide-mouthed jar, 1 gal. (4 liters)*
1 tea bag
pencil

Procedure
- *Fill the jar with water.*
- *Open the tea bag and pour the tea leaves into the water.*
- *Insert the pencil in the center of the water.*
- *Move the pencil quickly in a small circle until the tea leaves group and begin to swirl in the center area of the water.*

Results The tea leaves group in a spiraling funnel shape.

Why? The stirring creates a *vortex* in the jar (a mass of liquid or gas that whirls, forming a cavity in the center toward which things are pulled). The tea leaves are pulled toward the center of the vortex created by the rotating water. The red spot seen on Jupiter is a massive hurricane large enough to swallow three Earths. It is believed that red particles are swirled by moving gases as were the tea leaves, creating the massive storm that has not changed in appearance for as long as people have been able to view Jupiter.

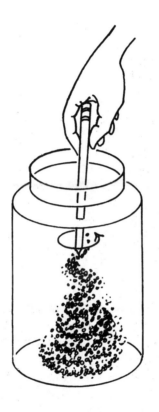

16. Glimmer

Purpose To determine why Jupiter's ring shines.

Materials *flashlight*
baby powder in a plastic shaker

Procedure
- *In a darkened room, place the flashlight on the edge of a table.*
- *Hold the open powder container below the beam of light.*
- *Quickly squeeze the powder container.*

Results The beam of light is barely visible before the powder is sprayed into it. After spraying powder into the light beam, the specks of powder glisten, making the light path visible.

Why? Light is not visible unless it can be reflected to your eye. The tiny specks of powder act like the fine particles in the ring around Jupiter in that they reflect the Sun's light. Jupiter's ring is 34,000 miles (54,400 km) from the planet's cloud tops. The material in these rings is thought to come from Io, the innermost of Jupiter's four large moons. Io is the only known moon with active volcanos, and it is possible that the ash from these volcanos forms Jupiter's ring.

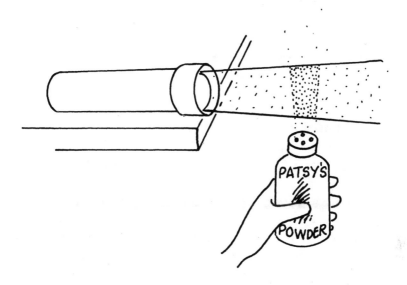

17. Hot

Purpose To determine if conservation of energy applies to friction between molecules in a dense atmosphere.

Materials *your hands*

Procedure
- *Place your palms together.*
- *Quickly rub your dry hands back and forth several times.*

Results Your dry hands feel hot when rubbed together.

Why? Friction between your hands produces heat energy, as does the friction between any moving objects. The closer the objects in motion are, the greater is the heat. This would make one think that the dense atmosphere around planets such as Jupiter would cause an increase in the surface temperature. The winds around Jupiter blow in excess of 896 miles (1,434 km) per hour. The atmospheric gases are constantly being rubbed together, but the temperature on the planet does not increase continuously. This supports the fact that in the collision between two molecules, the energy that one particle gains equals the energy lost by the other. The temperature on the planet Jupiter remains constant due to *conservation of energy.* Conservation of energy means that the heat, which is a measure of the total energy present, does not change. Any heat gained by one substance is equal to the heat lost by some other substance.

18. Hot and Cold

Purpose To determine how space acts as a heat shield for planets.

Materials *thermos bottle*
2 drinking cups
2 thermometers
wide-mouthed glass jar with a lid, 1 qt. (1 liter)
5 to 6 ice cubes
stirring spoon

Procedure

- *Fill the liter jar with hot water from the faucet.*
- *Place a thermometer in the jar for 2 minutes.*
- *Read and record the temperature of the hot water.*
- *Pour half of the water from the jar into the thermos.*
- *Close the lid on the thermos and on the jar.*
- *Allow the thermos and glass jar to sit undisturbed for 1 hour.*
- *Fill one of the cups with water from the thermos.*
- *Fill the second cup with water from the glass jar.*
- *Place one thermometer in each of the cups.*
- *Wait 2 minutes, then read and record the thermometer in each cup. Discard the water in the cups after reading the thermometers.*
- *Place the ice cubes inside the jar.*
- *Fill the jar with tap water and stir for about 15 seconds.*
- *Place a thermometer in the icy water for 2 minutes.*
- *Read and record the temperature of the cold water.*
- *Remove any unmelted ice, then pour half of the cold water into the thermos.*

- Secure the lids on the two containers and allow them to sit undisturbed for 1 hour.
- Fill one of the cups with water from the thermos.
- Fill the second cup with water from the glass jar.
- Again place one thermometer in each of the cups.
- Wait 2 minutes, then read and record the thermometer in each cup.

Results The temperature of the water inside the thermos changes less than does the water inside the glass jar.

Why? Heat from the hot water is transferred (conducted) to the glass and finally to the air. The cold water becomes warmer because a reverse movement of heat occurs: the heat from the air is transferred to the glass and then absorbed by the water. The materials inside the thermos are poor *conductors*. This means that heat travels through them very slowly. Between the poor conducting materials in the thermos is a partial *vacuum* (a space with almost no air). Heat has difficulty traveling through empty space, so the partial vacuum in the thermos as well as the space separating planets conducts very little heat. Both the thermos and the space around celestial bodies restrict the transfer of heat and can be said to act as a heat shield.

THERMOS —
QUART JAR

19. Charged

Purpose To determine why lightning continuously flashes on Jupiter.

Materials *wool cloth, use any 100% wool (coat, scarf, sweater, etc.)*
thin sheet of plastic (plastic report cover)
scissors

Procedure

- *Cut a plastic strip about 2 in. × 8 in. (5 cm × 20 cm).*
- *In a very dark room, hold the end of the plastic strip.*
- *Wrap the wool cloth around the plastic, then quickly pull the plastic through the cloth.*
- *Repeat this 5 or 6 times.*
- *Observe the cloth as you pull the plastic through it.*

Results A bluish light is seen in the folds of cloth that touch the plastic.

Why? Electrons are rubbed off the wool and onto the plastic strip. The wool becomes positively charged, causing the plastic to be negatively charged. When the electrons leap from the plastic back to the wool, an electric spark is seen.

Flashes of light are continuously seen through the clouds that swirl around the planet Jupiter. The molecules in the atmosphere are briskly rubbed together because of the winds that blow up to 800 miles (1,280 km) per hour. The rubbing of the molecules in the atmosphere, like the rubbing of the wool cloth on the plastic, results in electric sparks.

20. See Through

Purpose To determine how Saturn can be seen through its rings.

Materials *ruler*
white poster board
black marking pen
scissors
straight pin
pencil
glue

Procedure

- *Cut 3 strips from the poster board that are each 1 in. × 6 in. (2.5 cm × 15 cm).*
- *Evenly space the strips so that their centers cross.*
- *Glue the centers of the strips together.*
- *Use the marking pen to make two marks across the end of each strip. Start the first mark $1/2$ in. (1 cm) from the end of the strip and make the second mark 1 in. (2.5 cm) from the end.*
- *Insert the pin through the center of the strips. Work the pin to enlarge the hole so that the paper blades easily spin.*
- *Stick the end of the pin in a pencil eraser.*
- *Spin the paper blades.*
- *Observe the spinning blades.*

Results Two black rings are seen, but you can see through the spinning blades.

44

Why? Your eyes blend the color on the paper strips together as they spin, producing what appears to be solid rings. The rings around Saturn are not solid, but their movement makes them appear to be a continuous surface as does the movement of the black marks on the spinning paper. Saturn's rings are made of ice chunks and pieces of rock that range in size from house-size pieces to those as small as the head of a pin. The surface of Saturn is seen through the spaces between the spinning ice and rock chunks, just as you were able to see through the spaces between the paper as it turned.

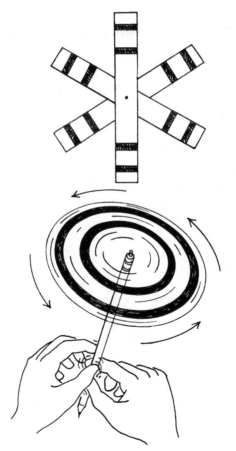

21. Shepherds

Purpose To determine how Saturn's moons affect the planet's rings.

Materials *record (one that can be scratched)*
sugar
2 pencils
masking tape
record player

Procedure

- *Tape 2 pencils together so that their points are even.*
- *Place the record on the turntable of the record player.*
- *Evenly cover the surface of the record with sugar.*
- *Hold the points of the pencils against the record.*
- *Spin the record around three times with your hand.*

Results As the record turns, the pencil points push the sugar to the side forming two cleared paths.

Why? Moons move within the chunks of ice that compose the rings around Saturn. It is believed that the moons herd the materials in the rings, keeping them in separate bands, as do the pencil points that move through the sugar crystals.

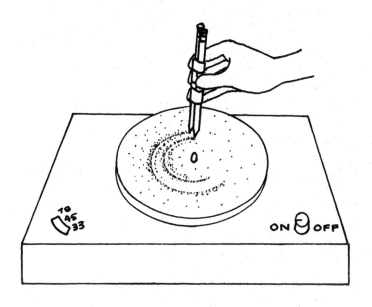

47

II
Space Movement

22. Curves

Purpose To demonstrate the effect of forces on orbital movement.

Materials pencil
2 chairs
yardstick (meter stick)
string
small paper cup
masking tape
scissors
salt
poster board (dark color)

Procedure

■ Separate the chairs and tape the ends of the yardstick to the top edge of each chair's back.

■ Cut two 1-yd. (1-m) lengths of string.

■ Attach both ends of one string to the yardstick to form a V-shaped support. Secure the ends with tape.

■ Loop the second string over the V-shaped string and use tape to attach the ends to the top rim of the cup, one on each side of the cup. Tie so that the cup is about 4 in. (10 cm) from the floor.

■ Lay the poster board under the hanging cup.

■ Fill the cup with salt.

■ Use the point of a pencil to make a small hole in the bottom of the cup.

■ Pull the cup back and release to allow it to swing forward.

Results The falling salt forms different patterns on the dark paper as the cup swings.

Why? The cup moves in different patterns because of the forces pulling on the cup. The cup was swung in a back and forth motion, the V-shaped support string pulled it in another direction, and there is the ever-present downward pull of gravity. Planets, like the cup, have different forces acting on them. Each planet spins on its axis and has a forward speed and is pulled on by other planets and its own moon(s), but the big pull is from the Sun. The combination of all of these forces guides the planet in the path (*orbit*) it takes around the Sun.

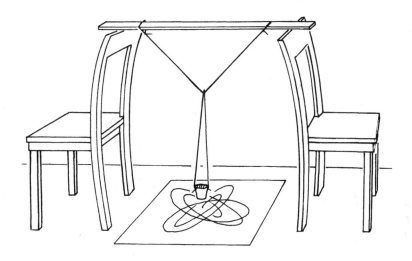

23. Speedy

Purpose To determine the effect of distance on the orbiting speed of planets.

Materials *1 metal washer*
        string

Procedure
Note: This activity is to be performed in an open, outside area away from other people.

- *Tie the washer to the end of a 1-yd. (1-m) length of string.*
- *Hold the end of the string and extend your arm outward.*
- *Swing your arm around so that the washer moves in a circular path beside your body.*
- *Spin the washer at the slowest speed necessary to keep the string taut.*
- *Hold the string in the center and again spin the washer at the slowest speed necessary to keep the string taut.*
- *Hold the string about 10 in. (25 cm) from the washer and spin as before.*

Results As the length of the string decreases, the washer must be spun around more times in order to keep the string taut.

Why? The washer seems to sluggishly move around in its circular path when attached to a long string, while on a shorter string, it zips around quickly. This slower and faster movement is real for planets that differ in their distance from the Sun. As the planet's distance from the Sun increases, the pull toward the Sun, called *gravity*, decreases. With less pull toward the Sun, the orbiting speed of the

52

planet decreases. Mercury, the closest planet to the Sun, has the fastest orbiting speed and Pluto, the furthermost planet, has the very slowest orbiting speed. (Twirling the washer on the string is not a true simulation of how planets move around the Sun, because the planets are not attached to the Sun by a cord.)

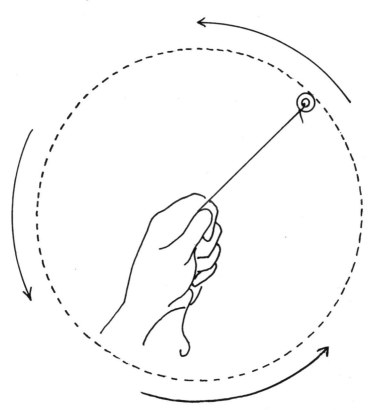

24. On the Move

Purpose To determine why planets continue to move.

Materials *round cake pan*
1 sheet construction paper
scissors
1 marble

Procedure

- *Use the cake pan to draw a circle on the paper.*
- *Cut the circle out.*
- *Place the pan on a flat surface.*
- *Lay the paper inside the pan and place the marble on top of the paper.*
- *Thump the marble so that it rolls around next to the wall of the pan.*
- *Remove the paper from the pan.*
- *Again thump the marble so that it rolls around next to the wall of the pan.*

Results The marble rolls in a circular path. It rolls farther and faster without the paper lining in the pan.

Why? *Inertia* is the resistance that an object has to any change in its motion. Inertia causes stationary objects to remain at rest and moving objects to continue to move in a straight line, unless some force acts on them. All objects have inertia. The marble has much less inertia than do larger objects such as celestial bodies like the Sun, the Moon, and planets, but they all resist a change in motion. The marble stopped moving quicker in the paper-lined pan because of *friction* (the rubbing of one object against another). When the friction between the pan and the marble was reduced, the marble rolled for a longer time. The planets continue to move around the Sun because their movement through space is not restricted by friction.

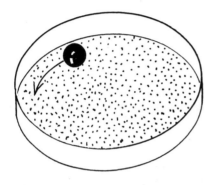

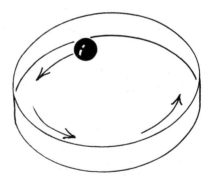

25. Spinner

Purpose To determine why planets move smoothly around the Sun.

Materials *ruler*
scissors
heavy, thick string
4 large paper clips
cardboard
sheet of paper
cake pan, 10-in. (25-cm) diameter
pencil

Procedure

■ *Use the cake pan to draw a circle on the paper and the cardboard.*

■ *Cut the circles out.*

■ *Fold the paper in half twice to find the center of the circle.*

■ *Lay the paper over the cardboard circle and make a hole through the center of both circles with the point of a pencil.*

■ *Discard the paper.*

■ *Cut a 1-yd. (1-m) length of string.*

■ *Thread one end of the string through the hole in the cardboard circle, and tie a knot on the other side to keep it from pulling back through.*

■ *Evenly space the 4 paper clips around the outer rim of the cardboard circle or disk.*

■ *Hold the end of the string and swing the disk back and forth.*

56

■ *Continue to hold the end of the string while you give the disk a quick spin toward you, then swing it as before.*

Results The disk flops around when merely moved around on the string, but when spun, it rotates in the plane in which it was originally spun.

Why? The cardboard disk acts like a gyroscope, a kind of top which when spinning stays pointed in one direction. The planets spin on their axis as they rotate around the Sun, this keeps them turning in the plane in which they were started just as the disk does.

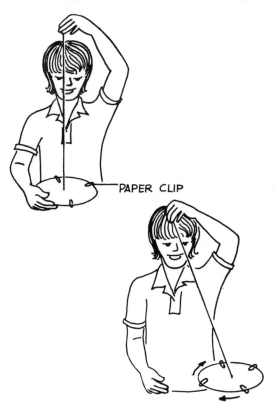

PAPER CLIP

26. Expanding

Purpose To demonstrate how galaxies may be moving.

Materials *round balloon, 9 in. (23 cm)*
black marking pen
mirror

Procedure

- *Inflate the balloon so that it is about as large as an apple.*
- *Use the marking pen to randomly make about 20 dots on the balloon.*
- *Stand in front of a mirror and observe the dots as you inflate the balloon.*

Results The dots move away from each other. Some seem to move farther than others, but no dots get closer together.

Why? Astronomers believe that the galaxies are moving away from each other similarly to the way the dots on the balloon move. Not all the galaxies are moving away from us at the same rate. In 1929, Dr. Edwin Hubble discovered that the farther away a galaxy is, the faster it seems to be moving away from us. Since no two galaxies seem to be getting closer as they move, scientists believe the universe is expanding.

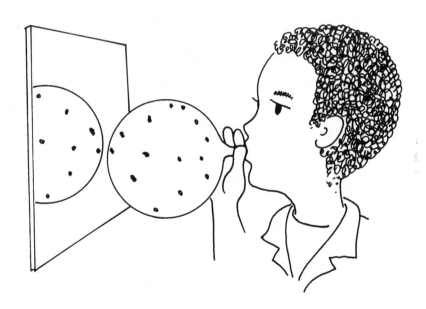

27. How Far?

Purpose To demonstrate how Neptune becomes the outermost planet.

Materials *tack board*
6 push tacks
string
pencil
scissors
ruler
paper

Procedure

- *Cut a piece of string 12 in. (30 cm) long.*
- *Tie the ends of the string together to form a loop that is about 6 in. (18 cm) long.*
- *Secure a piece of paper to the tack board with 4 tacks.*
- *Draw a line 5 in. (13 cm) long and stick a tack in each end of the line.*
- *Position the loop of string around the tacks.*
- *Place the pencil so that its point is against the inside of the loop.*
- *Keep the string taut as you guide the pencil around the inside of the string to draw an oval or ellipse on the paper.*
- *Cut an 8-in. (20-cm) length of string and tie the ends together to form a loop.*
- *Move the tacks and make new drawings until a position is found that produces a small ellipse inside the larger one with one end of the small ellipse overlapping the larger one.*

Results Two overlapping elliptical *orbits* are drawn.

Why? The orbits of all planets have an elliptical shape. Pluto's orbit overlaps the orbit of Neptune. It takes Pluto 248 years to make one trip around the Sun. During the journey, Pluto moves inside Neptune's orbit, making Neptune the outermost planet. Pluto last reached its *perihelion* (the point closest to the sun) in 1989.

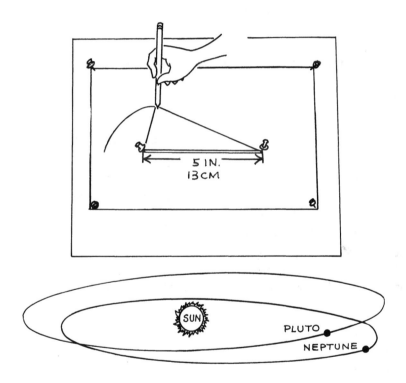

28. Balancing Point

Purpose To demonstrate the position of the Earth's *barycenter.*

Materials *scissors*
string
modeling clay
pencil
ruler

Procedure

- *Cut a 12-in. (30-cm) length of string.*
- *Tie the string about 1 in. (3 cm) from the end of the pencil.*
- *Make a ball of clay, about the size of a lemon.*
- *Stick the clay ball on the end of the pencil with the string.*
- *Mold the clay around the string so that the string is barely inside the edge of the clay ball.*
- *Add a grape-sized piece of clay to the opposite end of the pencil.*
- *Hold the end of the string and add small pieces of clay to the end of the pencil until the pencil balances horizontally.*

Results The pencil hangs in a horizontal position.

Why? The string is tied at the *center of gravity* —the point at which the weight of an object is evenly placed. Objects can be balanced at their center of gravity. The Moon and Earth move around the Sun like a single body. The center of gravity of the Earth-Moon system is called the *barycenter*. The barycenter is about 1044 miles (1670 km) beneath the Earth's surface on the side of Earth facing the Moon. The string represents the Earth's barycenter on the Earth-Moon model.

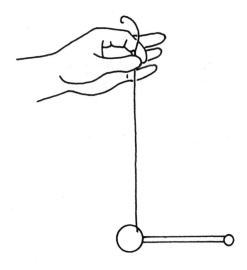

29. Lifter

Purpose To demonstrate how the atmosphere affects falling objects.

Materials *paper*
   book larger than the paper

Procedure
- *Position the paper on top of the book so that half of the paper is hanging over the edge of the book.*
- *Drop the book from a waist-high position.*
- *Observe the paper and book as they fall and strike the ground.*

Results The paper leaves the book and falls more slowly.

Why? Objects hit against air molecules as they fall. These air molecules push against the falling object causing its speed to decrease. The book's speed is not changed much because its weight (downward force) overcomes the resistance of the air in the Earth's atmosphere. The paper's weight equals the resistance of the air and thus falls at a slower speed. Since all objects fall at the same speed in a vacuum, the paper and the book would fall at the same speed on a planet with no atmosphere. This is due to the lack of resistance by gases in the atmosphere; the pull of gravity is the same on all objects, regardless of their mass. A thick atmosphere like that on Venus would cause the speed of both the paper and the book to decrease because the resistance by the atmospheric gases would be so much greater than on the Earth.

PAPER
BOOK

PHYSICS

65

30. Elliptical

Purpose To determine how gravity affects the movement of celestial bodies.

Materials *1 sheet of carbon paper*
1 sheet of typing paper
clipboard
modeling clay
cardboard tube from paper towel roll
large glass marble

Procedure

- *Place the typing paper on the clipboard.*
- *Lay the carbon paper on top of the typing paper, carbon side down.*
- *Place both sheets under the clip on the board.*
- *Raise the clip end of the board up by placing two marble-sized balls of clay under both corners.*
- *Place one end of the paper tube on top of the papers.*
- *The tube is to be parallel with the top of the clipboard.*
- *Slightly elevate the tube by placing a ball of clay under one end.*
- *Place the marble in the elevated end of the tube and allow it to roll out of the tube and across the papers.*
- *Raise the carbon sheet and observe the pattern produced on the typing paper.*

Results The pattern made by the marble is curved. *Note:* Change the elevation if the marble's path is not curved.

Why? The marble has a horizontal speed and would continue to move straight across the paper if gravity did not

66

pull it downward. The forward force plus the downward pull moves the marble in a curved path. The paths of planets are also affected by the gravitational pull of the Sun. All the planets have forward motions as well as a pull toward the Sun. If the Sun had no gravitational attraction, the planets would not orbit the Sun, but would move away from the Sun in a straight line.

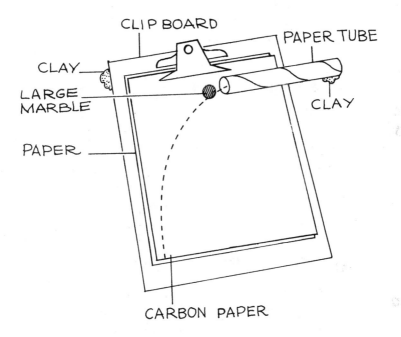

31. Satellite Crash

Purpose To demonstrate why a satellite stays in orbit.

Materials *large, empty, 3-lb. (1.4-kg) coffee can*
poster board
pencil
scissors
glass marble
masking tape

Procedure

- *On the poster board, draw a circle with a 22 in. (55 cm) diameter.*
- *Cut around the circle, then cut out a wedge (pie slice) that is one-eighth of the circle.*
- *Overlap the circle to form a cone that fits snugly in the coffee can with most of the cone sticking out the top of the can. Tape the cone so it does not open up.*
- *Tape the cone to the outside of the can.*
- *Roll the marble around the top of the cone as fast as possible and observe its movement.*

Results The marble rolls around the inside of the cone and its path begins to curve downward as the speed of the marble slows. The marble finally moves to the bottom of the cone and stops.

Why? The paper offers a continuous resistance to the movement of the marble, forcing it to move in a circular path, and gravity pulls the marble downward. As the forward speed of the marble decreases, the unchanging pull of gravity forces the marble to move down the cone toward the bottom. Satellites would continue to circle the Earth if they never lost their forward motion, but like the marble, as their speed decreases, gravity pulls them toward the Earth until finally they crash into the Earth. Planets and moons are examples of satellites since they all orbit another celestial body; they would crash if their forward speed decreased.

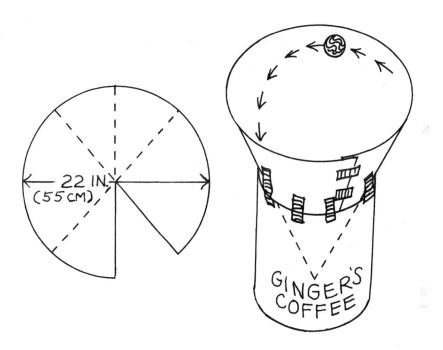

32. In and Out

Purpose To demonstrate forces that keep satellites in orbit.

Materials *masking tape*
metal spoon
thread spool
string
yardstick (meter stick)

Procedure

- *Cut 1 yd. (1 m) of string.*
- *Tie one end of the string to the roll of tape.*
- *Thread the free end of the string through the hole in the spool.*
- *Tie the spoon to the free end of the string.*
- *Hold the tape in one hand and hold the spool with your free hand.*
- *Give the spool a quick circular motion to start it spinning in a horizontal circle above your head.*
- *Release the tape and allow it to hang freely.*
- *Keep the spoon spinning by moving the thread spool in a circular motion.*
- *Observe the movement of the tape roll.*

Results The spoon spins in a circular path with only the weight of the tape pulling on the attached string.

Why? The tape pulls on the string and provides an inward force that keeps the spoon moving in a circular path. This force toward the center is called a *centripetal force*. Centripetal means center-seeking. If the force of the string were removed, the spoon would fly off in a straight line. Any circling object, spoon or satellite, has a centripetal force keeping it in its circular path. Moons that orbit planets and planets that orbit the Sun all are pulled toward the celestial body that they orbit. Their own forward speed keeps them from being pulled into the body that they orbit, and the centripetal force acting on the orbiting body keeps it from moving off into space.

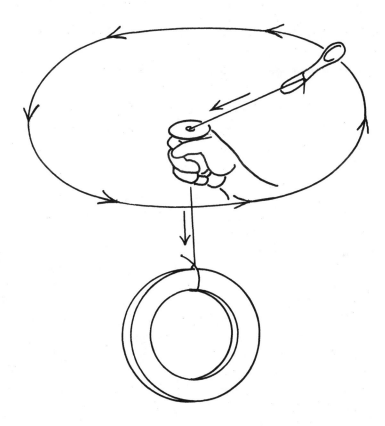

33. Same Place

Purpose To determine how satellites appear to be stationary.

Materials *rope about 3 yd. (3 m) long*
helper

Procedure

- *In an open area outside, use a tree or other object to represent the Earth.*
- *Ask your helper to hold one end of the rope as you hold on to the other end.*
- *Have your helper stand near the tree.*
- *Walk at a pace that keeps the rope tight and in a position so that you are in line with the same point on the tree as your helper.*

Results The person in the outside circle moves faster, but stays in line with the person moving in the smaller inside circle.

Why? The distance around the outside of the circle is larger than the circle near the tree. A faster speed is required to travel around the larger circle in the same time that the person travels around the smaller circle. Geostationary satellites are placed at about 22,500 miles (36,000 km) above the Earth. They have a very fast speed, which gives them an orbital period of 24 hours, the same as that of the Earth; the satellites thus appear to remain stationary above the Earth. There are more than 120 geostationary communications satellites positioned above the Earth's equator.

Two geostationary satellites located above the 75 and 135 degree longitudes provide a view of about one-third of the Earth's surface. These stationary satellites provide valuable weather information.

III

Sun

34. Radiate

Purpose To determine how heat from the Sun travels through space.

Materials *baseball cap*

Procedure

- *Stand outside in the direct sunlight.*
- *Face the direction of the Sun for 5 seconds.*
  Caution: NEVER look directly into the Sun because it can damage your eyes.
- *Position the cap on your head so that it shades your face.*
- *Stand with the cap on for 5 seconds.*
- *Remove the cap but remain in the same position for another 5 seconds.*

Results The skin on your face feels warmer without the cap.

Why? The Sun radiates light. Radiation is the process by which light is transferred by waves called visible light. These light waves travel at a speed of 186,000 miles per second (300,000 km per second) and move in straight lines. Because the light waves travel in straight lines, the brim of the cap was able to block the waves from your face. It took 8½ minutes for the light waves to travel the 93 milllion miles (149 million km) from the Sun to your skin, where they change to heat energy. Since the space between the Sun and the Earth is a near vacuum, light can travel through this emptiness only by means of waves, because no particles are required for their movement.

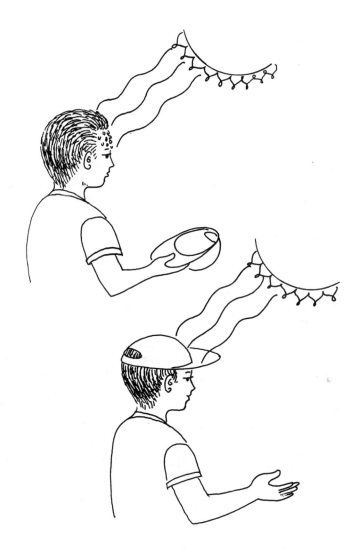

35. Blackout

Purpose To demonstrate a solar eclipse.

Materials *coin*

Procedure
- *Close one eye and look at a distant tree with your open eye.*
- *Hold a coin at arm's length in front of your open eye.*
- *Bring the coin closer to your open eye until it is directly in front of the eye.*

Results As the coin nears your face, less of the tree is seen until finally the tree is no longer visible.

Why? The coin is smaller than the tree, just as the Moon is smaller than the Sun, but they both are able to block out light when they are close to the observer. When the Moon passes between the Sun and the Earth, it blocks out light just like the coin. The blocking of the Sun's light by the Moon is called a *solar eclipse*. The Moon moves around the Earth about once a month, but a solar eclipse does not occur monthly. The Moon's orbit is not around the Earth's equator, and the Earth's axis is tilted, which causes the Moon's shadow to miss the surface of the Earth most of the time. A solar eclipse occurs three or fewer times per year.

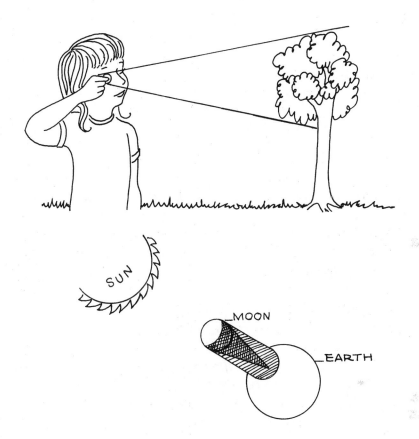

SUN

MOON

EARTH

79

36. Mini-Eclipse

Purpose To demonstrate a solar eclipse with a sundial.

Materials *ruler*
cardboard, 12 in. × 12 in. (30 cm × 30 cm)
pencil
masking tape
compass
watch
marking pen

Procedure

- *Draw a circle in the center of the cardboard square.*
- *Mark the letter N on the inside edge of the circle for north.*
- *Push the pencil through the center of the circle and tape it upright.*
- *Place the sundial in a sunny area outside.*
- *Use the compass to find north and turn the cardboard so that the N faces north.*
- *Mark the position of the center of the pencil's shadow on the circle and write the time there.*
- *Repeat the previous step several times during the day.*
- *Use the sundial to tell the time of day.*

Results The pencil casts a shadow across the circle at different points during the day. The shadow is darker in the center than on the outside.

Why? The pencil casts a shadow because light from the Sun travels in a straight line. The pencil blocks the Sun's light, forming a shadow on the paper. The darker part of the shadow is called the *umbra* and the lighter outer portion is called the *penumbra*. During a solar eclipse, the Moon blocks the Sun's light to form a shadow on the Earth. The shadow of the pencil changes position because the Earth rotates and the Sun's light strikes the pencil from a different angle. During a solar eclipse, the shadow of the Moon, like that of the pencil, falls on different areas of the Earth because of the Earth's rotation.

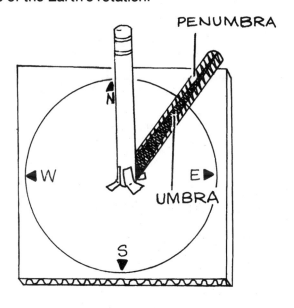

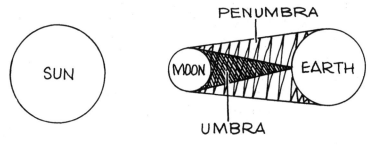

37. Shut Out

Purpose To demonstrate the effect a lunar eclipse has on studying the Sun's corona.

Materials *index card*
straight pin
desk lamp

Procedure
Caution: NEVER look at the Sun directly because it can damage your eyes.
- *Use the straight pin to make a hole in the center of the card.*
- *Slightly hollow out the hole so that you can see through it.*
- *Turn the lamp on.*
- *Close your right eye.*
- *Hold the card in front of your left eye.*
- *Look through the pinhole at the glowing lamp.*

Results The print on the outside of the bulb can be read when looking through the pinhole.

Why? The card shuts out most of the light from the bulb, allowing the print to be visible. During a solar eclipse, the Moon blocks the glaring light from the Sun, allowing the less intense glowing outer surface, or *corona,* to be studied.

PINHOLE

60 WATT

38. Swirls

Purpose To determine the color composition of sunlight.

Materials *clear, plastic ballpoint pen*
1 sheet typing paper

Procedure
- *Place the paper on a table near a window so that it receives the morning sunlight.*
- *Lay the pen on the paper so that the Sun's light hits directly on it.*
- *Roll the pen back and forth on the paper very slowly.*

Results Swirls of colors appear in the shadow made by the pen.

Why? The clear plastic acts like a prism and breaks the white light of the Sun into its separate colors of red, orange, yellow, green, blue, indigo, and violet. You may not see each of these colors, but you can determine that there is a definite order of colors ranging from red to blue.

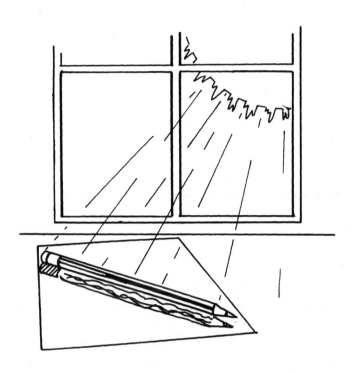

39. Clock Compass

Purpose To demonstrate how a clock can be used as a compass.

Materials *1 sheet notebook paper*
straight pin
compass
ruler
scissors
cardboard, 12 in. × 12 in. (30 cm ×
*   30 cm)*
pencil
clock

Procedure

- *Cut a 6-in. (15-cm) diameter circle from the paper.*
- *Write the numbers on the paper circle as they appear on a clock.*
- *Lay the paper circle in the center of the cardboard.*
- *Stick a straight pin vertically in the center of the paper circle.*
- *Place the cardboard on an outside surface in direct sunlight.*
- *Turn the paper circle until the shadow of the pin falls on the correct time. Do not use daylight savings time.*

Results North will be halfway between the shadow and the number 12 on your paper clock.

Note: Use a compass to check the accuracy of your clock compass.

Why? This compass is most accurate March 21 and September 23 when the Sun rises in the east and sets in the west. On these dates, the shadow of the pin approaches due north as noon nears. At other times of the year, the clock compass loses accuracy, but the general direction of north can be found.

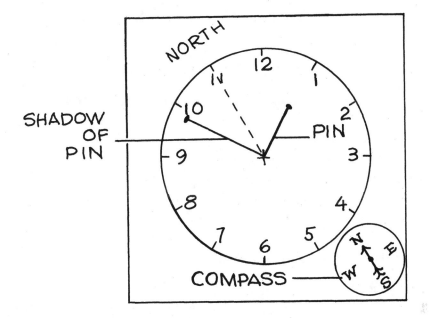

40. Waves

Purpose To simulate the presence of planets with magnetic fields.

Materials *iron filings, as found in magnetic disguise games*
small magnet, round or bar-shaped
sheet of paper
string
scissors
masking tape
ruler

Procedure

- *Cut a 6-in. (15-cm) length of string.*
- *Secure the string to the magnet with tape.*
- *Place the magnet on a table and cover it with a sheet of paper.*
- *Spread a thin layer of iron filings on top of paper.*
- *Slowly pull on the string to move the magnet under the paper.*

Results The iron filings form a pattern on the paper above the magnet. As the magnet moves, the iron filings move.

Why? A force field exists around all magnets that can move magnetic materials such as iron filings. As the magnet moves, the iron filings are moved by this *magnetic force field*. The Earth has a magnetic force field that affects the iron needle in a compass. The Earth deflects any radioactive particles in its path because of its magnetic force field. These particles are emitted from solar flares. The defection of these particles by other planets as they move around the Sun is a clue that those planets also have magnetic fields.

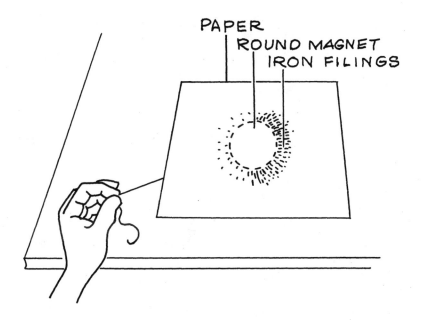

PAPER

ROUND MAGNET

IRON FILINGS

41. Mirage

Purpose To determine why the Sun's image is seen before sunrise and after sunset.

Materials *small bowl that you can see through*
modeling clay
coin
water
helper

Procedure

- *Press a clay ball the size of a walnut into the center of the small bowl.*
- *Stick the coin in the center of the clay.*
- *Place the bowl near the edge of a table.*
- *Stand near the table so that you can see the entire coin.*
- *Slowly move backwards until the coin is just barely out of sight.*
- *Ask your helper to fill the bowl with water.*

Results The coin is visible and appears to be in a different position in the bowl.

Why? Light from the coin changes direction as it leaves the water and enters the air. This makes the coin appear to be in a different place. This change in the direction of light is called *refraction*. The Earth's atmosphere refracts light in a similar way, causing the image of the Sun to appear before the actual Sun rises above the horizon. The Sun's image also lingers after the Sun moves below the horizon at sunset.

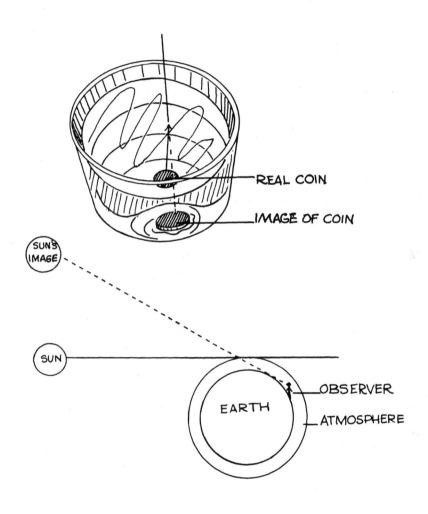

REAL COIN

IMAGE OF COIN

SUN'S IMAGE

SUN

OBSERVER

EARTH

ATMOSPHERE

42. Direct

Purpose To determine why Mars and Earth both have cold poles.

Materials *2 sheets of black construction paper*
2 thermometers
2 books
masking tape

Procedure

- *Tape one piece of black paper on each side of the book.*
- *Turn the book so that one sheet of paper receives direct sunlight.*
- *Tape a thermometer on top of each sheet of black paper.*
- *Read the temperature on both thermometers after 10 minutes.*

Results The thermometer facing the Sun has a higher temperature.

Why? The black paper facing the Sun receives more rays of Sun than the sheet on the opposite side of the book. Areas that receive direct rays from the Sun are much hotter. The Earth's equator receives about 2½ times as much heat during the year as does the area around the poles. Mars, like the Earth, has colder pole areas. Both of these planets are slightly tilted, causing the center to receive more direct solar rays than do the poles.

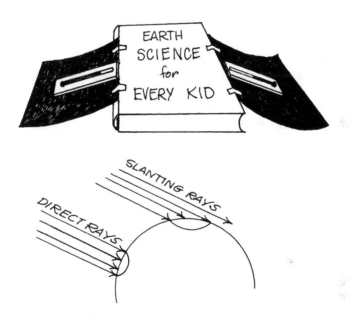

43. Sun Camera

Purpose To determine the size of the Sun.

Materials *1 sheet of paper*
yardstick (meter stick)
masking tape
pencil
1 index card
straight pin

Procedure

- *Draw two parallel lines on the sheet of paper about the thickness of the pencil lead apart.*
- *Punch a hole in the center of the index card with the straight pin.*
- *Fold one edge of the card and tape the folded edge to the zero end of the yardstick.*
- *Hold the paper at the 8 1/2-in. (218-mm) mark.*
- *Stand so that the shadow of the card falls on the paper.*
- *Look carefully at the paper and locate the small circle of light.*
  Caution: NEVER look directly into the Sun because it can damage your eyes.
- *Move the paper so that the circle of light fills the space between the lines on the sheet.*

Results The image of the Sun fits between the parallel lines on the paper.

Why? The distance from the hole in the card to the paper is 109 times the width (diameter) of the circle of light on the paper. Dividing the distance from the hole in the card to the paper by 109 will result in the diameter of the circle.

distance ÷ 109 = diameter
8 ½ in. ÷ 109 = thickness of the pencil lead
218 mm ÷ 109 = 2 mm

The distance from the Earth to the Sun is 109 times the Sun's diameter. Astronomers have determined the distance from Earth to the Sun to be about 93,750,000 miles (150,000,000 km). Dividing the distance to the Sun by 109 will give the diameter of the Sun:

distance ÷ 109 = diameter
93,750,000 mi. ÷ 109 = 86,009 mi. (137,614.4 km)

44. Distortion

Purpose To determine how the atmosphere affects the viewed shape of the Sun.

Materials *pencil*
> *sheet of notebook paper*
> *magnifying lens*

Procedure

■ *In the center of the paper, draw a circle with about a 1-in. (2.5-cm) diameter.*

■ *Look through the magnifying lens at the circle.*

■ *Move the lens back and forth as you view the circle.*

Results The shape of the circle becomes distorted.

Why? The glass in the magnifying lens has different thicknesses. As light passes through the lens, it changes directions. This change of the light's direction is called *refraction*. The thicker the lens, the more the light is refracted. A *mirage* (image that is not real) is seen due to refraction of light. The apparent flattening of the Sun at dusk, when it is near the horizon, is due to refraction of light. The rays from the bottom edge of the Sun are closer to the horizon and therefore travel through more of the Earth's atmosphere than the rays from the top edge of the Sun. These rays bend toward the Earth as they travel through the thicker section of the atmosphere. The atmosphere, like the magnifying lens, changes the direction of light passing through it, thus distorting the image seen.

Caution: Be very careful not to look directly at the Sun when confirming this experiment. Even the setting Sun can burn your delicate retina.

45. Trapped

Purpose To determine how the Earth is protected from solar winds.

Materials *drinking straw*
2 sheets of notebook paper
bar magnet
iron filings, as found in magnetic disguise
games

Procedure
■ *Cover the magnet with one sheet of paper.*
■ *Fold the second sheet of paper and sprinkle iron filings in the fold.*
■ *Hold the paper about 6 in. (15 cm) from the magnet.*
■ *Blow through the straw.*
■ *Direct the stream of air at the iron filings in the folded paper. A stream of iron filings are blown toward the magnet.*

Results Particles of iron stick to the paper in the shape of the underlying magnet.

Why? Around the magnet is a *magnetic force field* that attracts the iron filings. The Earth has a magnetic force field surrounding it. The area affected by the magnetic field is called the *magnetosphere.* The magnetosphere deflects and traps charged particles from the Sun, much as the magnet under the paper attracted the iron filings. The charged particles come from the Sun as a result of solar flares and sunspots. These moving particles are called solar winds and reach the Earth's orbit at speeds up to 1 to 2 million miles/hr (1.6 to 3.2 million km/hr). Astronauts in space could be in danger from solar flare particles because the high energy particles damage living tissue. Without the Earth's magnetosphere, living organisms on the Earth would be in danger from the charged particles.

46. Sky Path

Purpose To demonstrate the apparent path of the Sun across the sky.

Materials *pencil*
round glass bowl, 2 qt. (2 liter)
sheet of white paper
marking pen
compass

Procedure

- *Mark an X in the center of the paper.*
- *Place the paper outside in direct sunlight.*
- *Turn the bowl upside down on the paper with the X in the center of the bowl.*
- *Touch the glass dome with the tip of the pencil so that the shadow of the pencil's tip falls on the X mark.*
- *With the marking pen, make a dot on the glass where the tip of the pencil touches the glass.*
- *Continue to make marks every hour throughout the day.*
- *Use a compass to determine the direction of the Sun's movement.*

Results A curved path starting in the eastern sky and ending in the western sky is marked on the glass as the Sun appears to move across the sky.

Why? The Sun is not moving from east to west, but rather the Earth is turning toward the east. The Earth rotates once every 24 hours, giving the illusion that the Sun rises in the east, reaches its highest point in the sky at noon, and then begins to sink in the western sky. Because the Earth is tilted, the Sun actually rises due east and sets due west only during spring and fall months. In the winter months, the Sun rises in the southeast and sets in the southwest. In the summer months, the Sun rises in the northeast and sets in the northwest.

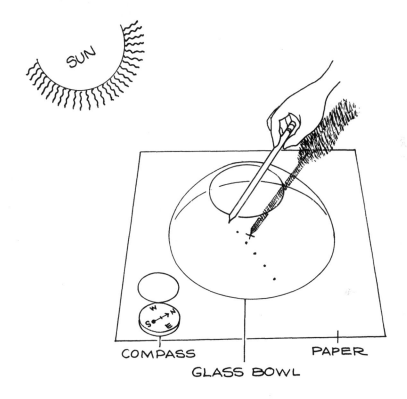

COMPASS   PAPER

GLASS BOWL

IV
Moon

47. Night Lights

Purpose To simulate and describe the attraction of charged particles near the Earth's poles.

Materials *paper hole punch*
tissue paper
round balloon, small enough to hold in your hand when inflated
your own hair —be sure it is clean, dry, and oil-free

Procedure

- *Punch 20 to 30 holes out of the tissue paper with the hole punch.*
- *Place the paper circles on a table.*
- *Stroke the balloon against your hair 10 times.*
- *Hold the stroked side of the balloon near, but not touching, the paper circles.*

Results The paper circles jump toward the balloon. Some of the circles leap off of the balloon.

Why? The paper circles represent charged particles circling the Earth at great distances, and the balloon represents the Earth. As was explained in Experiment 45, the Earth has a *magnetosphere* around it that deflects and traps charged particles from the Sun. The poles of the Earth act like strong magnets and pull some of the charged particles from the magnetosphere toward the Earth. Unlike the paper circles, the charged particles do not hit and leap from the Earth's surface, but move around in the upper atmosphere near the poles bumping into the atoms of gas in

104

the atmosphere. The gas atoms become excited when hit by these charged particles and release visible light. Each type of atom emits a specific color, resulting in a spectacular light display. The light display in the Northern Hemisphere is called an *aurora borealis* and in the Southern Hemisphere an *aurora australis.*

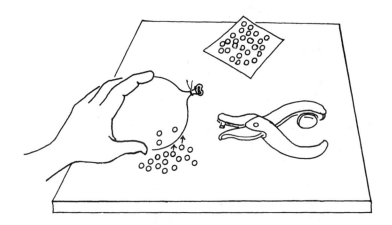

48. Moving Target

Purpose To simulate aiming a spacecraft for the Moon.

Materials *string*
ruler
washer
scissors
1 sheet of paper toweling
book
masking tape

Procedure

- *Cut a string 24 in. (60 cm) long.*
- *Tape one end of the string to the end of the ruler.*
- *Tie the washer to the free end of the string.*
- *Place the ruler on a table with about 4 in. (10 cm) of the ruler extending over the edge of the table.*
- *Place a book on the ruler to secure it to the table.*
- *Tear and wad up 10 small grape-sized pieces of paper toweling.*
- *Pull the hanging washer to the side and release to start it swinging.*
- *Sit about 1 yd. (1 m) from the swinging washer.*
- *Pitch one wad of paper at a time at the moving washer.*
- *Record the number of paper wads that hit the swinging washer.*

Results You may have been unsuccessful in hitting the washer. If so, try again.

Why? It is difficult to hit a moving target with a moving object. It takes time for the paper wads to move through the air. While they move, the washer moves to another position. This experiment simulates the problem that spacecraft have when traveling to the Moon. At point A on the diagram, the spacecraft must decide on a direction that will bring it to the Moon. If the craft follows a straight course as indicated by the dashed lines, it will be heading toward the Moon. But the Moon does not stand still; it orbits the Earth at a speed of 2,000 miles (3,200 km) per hour. Before the craft reaches point A, the Moon will have moved to point B. Astronauts know how long it takes the Moon and the space craft to arrive at different points on the Moon's orbital path. The craft must be aimed at a point where the Moon and the craft will meet or coincide. You must direct the paper wads to a point in front of the moving washer so that, like the spacecraft and the Moon, your paper wad and the washer arrive at the same place at the same time.

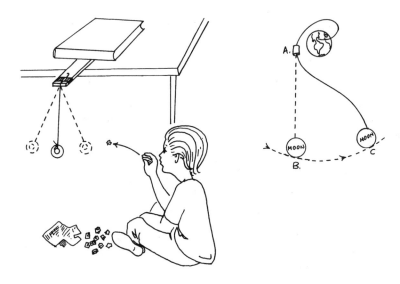

49. Moonbeams

Purpose To demonstrate the time it takes light from the Moon to reach the Earth. Compare the speed of light to the speed of a human.

Materials *stop watch*
2 helpers
2 pencils
yardstick (meter stick)

Procedure

- *Ask one of the helpers to be the official timekeeper who will indicate a starting time and a stopping time of 4 seconds.*
- *The second helper is to watch and determine your position at the end of the 4 seconds.*
- *Lay the pencil on the ground to mark the starting position.*
- *Stand at the starting position.*
- *When the timekeeper says START, run forward as fast as you can.*
- *Stop when the timekeeper says STOP at the end of 4 seconds.*
- *Your second helper will place a pencil to mark your position at the end of 4 seconds.*
- *Use a yardstick (meter stick) to measure the distance.*
- *Divide the distance by 3.*

Results Dividing the distance traveled by 3 gives the distance you traveled in one-third the time (4 seconds ÷ 3 = 1⅓ seconds).

108

Results for the author of this book:

> Total Distance ÷ 3 = Distance traveled in 1⅓ seconds
> 21 yd. (19.2 m) ÷ 3 = 7 yd. (6.4 m)

Why? 1⅓ seconds is the time it takes light to travel from the Moon to the Earth. The author raced across her yard at a rate of 7 yd. (6.4 m) in 1⅓ seconds while moonbeams of light sped toward the Earth at a spectacular speed of about 419,942,400 yd. (384,000,000 m) in the same 1⅓ seconds.

50. Shiner

Purpose To demonstrate why the Moon shines.

Materials *bicycle reflector*
flashlight

Procedure

- *Do this experiment at night.*
- *Point the flashlight at a bicycle reflector.*
- *Turn the flashlight off.*

Results The reflector only glows when the flashlight is on.

Why? The reflector does not give off light. It is designed to reflect light in different directions. The Moon is not a luminous body (one that gives off its own light). The Moon only reflects light from the Sun. Without the Sun, there would be no moonlight.

51. Spinner

Purpose To demonstrate why the Moon stays in orbit.

Materials *paper plate*
scissors
marble

Procedure
- *Cut the paper plate in half and use one side.*
- *Place the marble on the cut edge of the plate.*
- *Set the plate down on a table and slightly tilt it so that the marble moves quickly around the groove in the plate.*

Results The marble leaves the plate and moves in a straight line away from the paper plate.

Why? Objects move in a straight path unless some force pushes or pulls on them. The marble moved in a circular path while on the plate because the paper continued to push the marble toward the center of the plate. As soon as the paper ended, the marble traveled in a straight line. The Moon has a forward speed and, like the marble, would move off in a straight line if the gravitational pull toward the Earth did not keep it in its circular path.

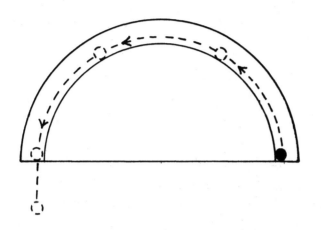

52. Changes

Purpose To determine why the Moon appears and disappears.

Materials *styrofoam ball the size of an apple*
pencil
lamp

Procedure

- *Insert the pencil in the styrofoam ball.*
- *Position the lamp near a doorway.*
- *Stand in a darkened room facing the lighted doorway.*
- *Hold the ball in front of you and slightly higher than your head.*
- *Slowly turn yourself around. Keep the ball in front of you as you turn.*
- *Observe the ball as you turn.*

Results The ball is dark when you face the door. Part of the ball lightens as you turn and is fully illuminated when your back is to the door. The ball starts to darken as you turn toward the door.

Why? The light from the doorway lights up one side of the ball at a time—the side facing the lamp. As you turn, more of the lighted side faces you. The Moon behaves like the ball. Moon light is a reflection of the Sun's light, and only one side of the Moon faces the Sun. The Moon has phases because as the Moon travels around the Earth different parts of its bright side are seen.

53. Plop!

Purpose To determine how craters are formed by falling meteorites.

Materials newspaper (about 25 sheets)
2 sheets of carbon paper
2 sheets of typing paper
1 golf ball

Procedure
- Fold the newspaper sheets in half and place them on the floor.
- Lay one sheet of typing paper on top of the newspaper.
- Place the carbon paper on top of the typing paper (carbon side down).
- Stand at the edge of the newspaper and bounce the golf ball on the carbon paper several times.
- Place the second sheet of typing paper on a hard floor.
- Place the carbon paper on top of the typing paper (carbon side down).
- Stand at the edge of the papers and bounce the golf ball on the carbon paper several times.
- Examine both pieces of typing paper.

Results The dimples on the golf ball made imprints on the typing paper. More dimples were made when the paper was on the softer newspaper backing than when it was on the hard floor.

Why? When the ball hits the paper, the carbon is pressed onto the white paper. The ball is round and only a small part of the surface touches the paper. The softer surface allowed more of the ball to be touched by the white paper. Holes, called craters, are formed when meteorites strike the powdery surface of the Moon. The Apollo explorations revealed that the lunar landscapes are covered by a layer of fine powder and rubble about 3 to 60 ft. (1 to 20 m) deep. The soft layer is called the lunar soil even though, unlike the soil on the Earth, it contains no water or organic materials. Astronomers have counted about 30,000 craters on the Moon. They range in size from microscopic craters 1/25,000 of an inch (1/1000 of a millimeter) in diameter produced by tiny particles of cosmic dust to 10 miles (16 km) with depths up to 2 miles (3 km). The largest craters can be seen with ordinary field glasses.

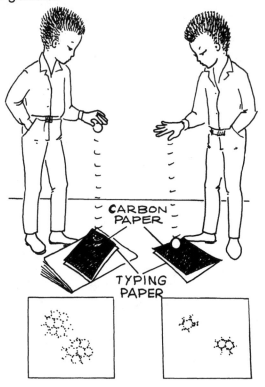

CARBON PAPER

TYPING PAPER

54. Face Forward

Purpose To demonstrate that the Moon rotates on its axis.

Materials *2 sheets of paper*
marker
masking tape

Procedure

■ *Draw a circle in the center of one sheet of paper.*

■ *Write the word EARTH in the center of the circle, and place the paper on the floor.*

■ *Mark a large X in the center of the second sheet of paper, and tape this paper to a wall.*

■ *Stand by the side of the paper on the floor and face the X on the wall.*

■ *Walk around the Earth, but continue to face the X.*

■ *Turn so that you face the paper labeled EARTH.*

■ *Walk around the Earth, but continue to face the Earth.*

Results Facing the X-marked paper resulted in different parts of your body pointing toward the paper marked EARTH as you revolved around the Earth. Continuing to face the Earth allowed only your front side to point toward the Earth during the revolution.

Why? You had to turn your body slightly in order to continue to face the Earth as you moved around it. In order for the same side of the Moon to always face the Earth, the Moon also has to turn slowly on its axis as it moves around the Earth. The Moon rotates one complete turn on its own axis during the 28 days it takes to revolve around the Earth.

55. Heavy

Purpose To demonstrate the effect of the Moon's gravity on weight.

Materials *marker*
masking tape
2 rubber bands
string
large rock
large cooking pot or bucket
string
scissors

Procedure

■ *Tie the rubber bands together.*

■ *Tie a string around the rock and attach the string to the rubber bands.*

■ *Place the cooking pot on a table.*

■ *Set the rock in the bottom of the pot.*

■ *Hold the free end of the rubber band and gently lift the rock just above the bottom of the pot.*

■ *Observe the length of the rubber bands.*

■ *Fill the pot with water.*

■ *Set the rock in the pot.*

■ *Hold the rubber band and lift the rock just above the bottom of the pot.*

■ *Observe the length of the rubber bands.*

Results The length of the rubber bands needed to support the rock decreased when water was poured into the pot.

Why? *Gravity* pulls down on the rock, causing the attached rubber bands to stretch. Adding water to the pot decreases the downward pull. The water pushes up on the rock, canceling some of the downward pull of gravity. The pull of gravity through the water simulates the reduced gravity on our Moon. The rubber bands would stretch even less if the rock were picked up on the Moon, because the Moon's gravity is only one-sixth that of the Earth's gravity.

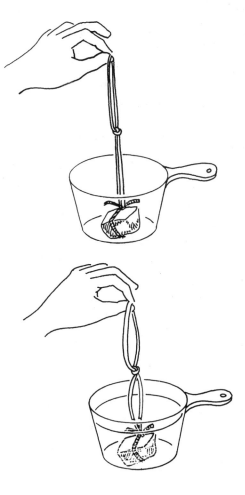

56. Faces

Purpose To determine the cause of the "Man in the Moon" image.

Materials *dominoes*
flashlight

Procedure
- *Stand 6 to 8 dominoes on a table.*
- *Darken the room and hold a flashlight at an angle about 12 in. (30 cm) from the dominoes.*

Results The dominoes form shadows on the table.

Why? The dominoes block the light from the flashlight much as the mountainous regions on the Moon, called *highlands,* block the Sun's light. The shadows of the highlands fall across the flat plains, called *maria.* The highlands look brighter, as they reflect the light, and the maria look darker because of the shadows. The insides of craters on the Moon also appear dark. The combination of highlands, maria, and craters forms the "Man in the Moon" pattern on the surface of the Moon.

57. Splatter

Purpose To determine why Moon craters are different from those on the planet Mercury.

Materials *plate*
bowl, 2 qt. (2 liter)
spoon
dirt

Procedure

- *Fill the bowl one-half full with dirt.*
- *Add small amounts of water, stirring continuously, until a muddy mixture is formed that slowly drips off of the tilted spoon.*
- *Fill the plate with the mud mixture.*
- *Shake the plate to smooth the surface of the mud.*
- *Allow mud to drop from the tilted spoon held about 24 in. (60 cm) above the plate.*
- *Move the spoon so that the mud drips back onto different areas of the mud's surface.*

Results The mud splashes and produces craterlike indentations.

Why? The falling mud hits the wet surface and the liquid splatters. The Earth's *gravity* pulls the liquid back to the surface, forming separate crater-shaped indentations where each drop of mud struck the surface. The falling mud simulates meteorites striking a surface. The tremendous amounts of heat produced by the impact of large meteorites melt the surface, and the liquid lava produces splatters, as did the mud. It is the rate at which the liquid fell that caused the difference between the crater formations on Mercury and those on the Moon. The separate craters with smooth planes between each crater observed on Mercury may be due to the planet's greater gravitational pull. The lava thrown upward by the impact of the meteorite would have moved a short distance then quickly pulled back to the surface with very little outward spreading of the material. The decreased gravity on the Moon allowed the liquid to be blown higher and with more fanning out. The lava on the Moon spread over a larger area, and thus the rims of many of the craters overlap, and the craters are separated by rough areas where thin layers of the lava fell on the surface.

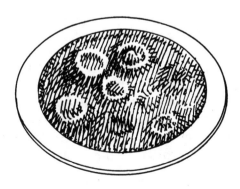

58. Too Much

Purpose To determine why the Moon's daytime temperature is so high.

Materials *sheet of black construction paper*
desk lamp
2 thermometers
timer

Procedure

■ *Lay the black paper under the lamp.*

■ *Place both thermometers on the black paper with the lamp about 4 in. (10 cm) from the bulbs of the thermometers.*

■ *Record both temperatures after 5 minutes.*

■ *Remove one of the thermometers and place it away from the lamp for 5 minutes.*

■ *Record the temperature on both thermometers.*

Results The reading on the thermometer that remained under the lamp is much higher than on the thermometer that was moved.

Why? The continuous heating of the air and paper under the lamp was recorded by the thermometer that remained there. The second thermometer was moved from a heated area to a cooler area and its reading was lower. The Moon's daytime temperature is about 266°F (+130°C). This is because the Sun shines on the Moon's surface continuously for about two Earth weeks. There is also very little protection from the solar rays because the Moon's *gravity* is so weak that a protective atmosphere cannot be captured as it has around the Earth. It takes 29½ days for the Moon to rotate on its own axis, compared to 24 hours for the Earth to make one turn. This slow turning allows the Sun to beat on the unprotected surface, heating the rocks to temperatures above the boiling point for water. While the sunny side is cooking, the shaded side is being exposed to very cold space. The shady side of the Moon cools to about − 279.4°F (− 173°C).

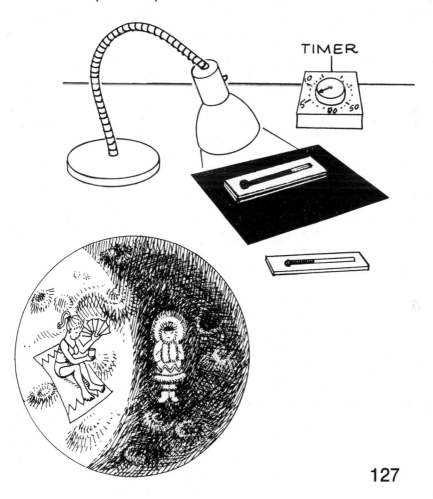

TIMER

V
Stars

59. Star Clock

Purpose To determine why the stars seem to move in circles across the night sky.

Materials *umbrella, solid, dark color*
white chalk

Procedure

- *Use chalk to draw the stars in the Big Dipper on one of the panels inside the umbrella. Draw the entire constellation.*
- *Hold the umbrella over your head.*
- *Turn the handle slowly in a counterclockwise direction.*

Results The center of the umbrella stays in the same place, and the stars move around.

Why? The stars in the constellation called the Big Dipper appear to move around a central star like hands on a backward clock. The stars make one complete turn every 24 hours, but unlike a clock, the hands are not in the same position each night at the same time. The stars reach a given position about 4 minutes earlier each night. Actually, the stars are not moving, we are. The Earth makes one complete rotation every 24 hours, making the stars appear to move. The axis of the Earth points to Polaris, the North Star, and it is this star that all the other stars appear to move around.

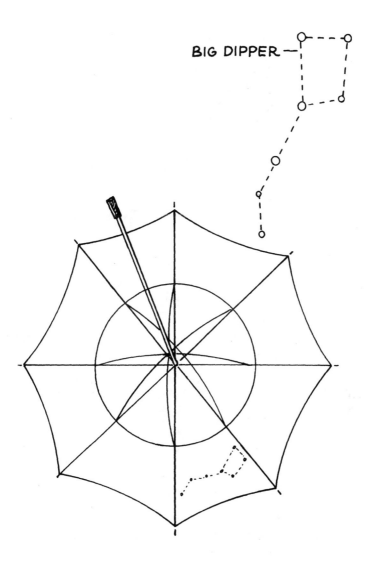

BIG DIPPER —

60. Shrinking

Purpose To determine how a black hole might be formed.

Materials 2 balloons, use a small, round size
2 large-mouthed glass jars
refrigerator
marking pen

Procedure

■ Prepare two separate jars with balloons inflated inside each.

■ Hold each balloon so that its mouth is above the edge of the jar and the remaining part of the balloon is inside the jar.

■ Inflate the balloons inside the jars.

■ Tie the openings of the balloons closed.

■ Mark the balloons just above the top edge of the jars with the marking pen.

■ Place one jar in the freezer for 30 minutes and place the second jar on a table so that it remains at room temperature.

■ After 30 minutes, remove the jar from the freezer.

■ Observe the position of the mark on both balloons.

Results The balloon at room temperature remains unchanged, but chilling the balloon caused it to shrink and sink into the jar.

Why? Gas inside the balloon pushes out and the elastic balloon pushes in. The size of the balloon remains the same as long as the pressure inside and out are equal. The balloon shrank when the inside pressure decreased. If the inside pressure continued to decrease, the force of the elastic material would cause the balloon to become smaller and smaller. It is the balance between the pressure of the elastic pushing in and the inside gases pushing out that can explain the formation of a black hole. The nuclear reactions at the center of a star produce an outward pressure. As long as the gravity of the star pulling in equals this outward pressure, the star, like the balloon, remains stable in size. When the nuclear reactions stop, the balance between gravity and the outward force is upset, and gravity pulls the star's materials toward the center of the star. It is believed that the shrinking could continue until the star becomes so small that it would no longer be visible, and thus a black hole would be formed.

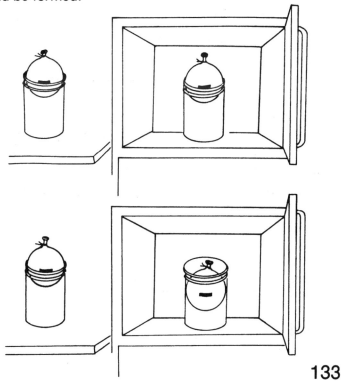

61. Distant Stars

Purpose To determine which star is closest to the Earth.

Materials *your thumb*
modeling clay
pencil

Procedure

- *Use the modeling clay to hold the pencil in a vertical position on a table.*
- *Stand across the room and hold your thumb at arm's length in front of your face.*
- *Close your left eye.*
- *Using your right eye, sight across the tip of your thumb at the pencil eraser.*
- *Do not move your head or your thumb. Close your right eye and use your left eye to look at the tip of your thumb.*
- *Notice the distance your thumb seems to move when you switch eyes.*
- *Hold your thumb at the end of your nose and again use your right eye to sight across the tip of your thumb at the pencil eraser.*
- *Do not move your thumb or your head. Look at your thumb tip with your left eye. Notice how far your thumb seems to move.*

Results Switching from the right to the left eye seems to make the thumb move. The movement is greater when the thumb is closer to the eyes.

Why? The thumb appears to move because it is being viewed from different angles. The movement is greatest

134

when the thumb is closest to the face. A star close to the Earth has an apparent change in its position when viewed from different sides of the Earth's orbit. During the winter, an observer from Earth would see star A behind the close star, but during the summer, star B appears behind the close star. This is because the close star is being viewed from different angles; this apparent movement is called *stellar parallax*. When comparing the stellar parallax of two different stars, the one that seems to move the most will be the star closest to the Earth.

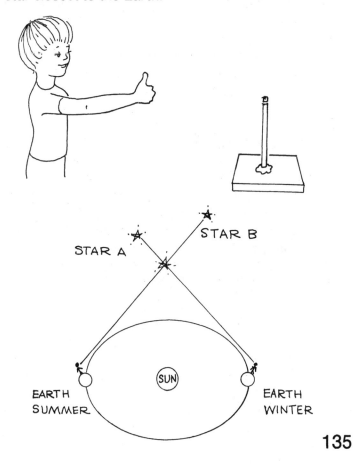

STAR B

STAR A

SUN

EARTH
SUMMER

EARTH
WINTER

62. Spreader

Purpose To demonstrate how distance affects a star's apparent brightness.

Materials *flashlight*

Procedure

■ *Stand in the center of a darkened room and shine the flashlight at a wall.*

■ *Slowly walk toward the wall and observe the light pattern produced on the wall.*

Results The light pattern becomes brighter and smaller in size as the flashlight nears the wall.

Why? Light moves away from the flashlight in a straight line. If the beam of light leaves the light source at an angle, it continues to spread out until it hits an object. Other light sources, such as stars, behave in the same manner. Two stars giving off the same amount of light, but at different distances from the Earth, will appear to have different magnitudes (degrees of brightness). The spreading of the light from the most distant star results in less light hitting the Earth. Thus the distant star appears dimmer, as did the light when the flashlight was farthest from the wall.

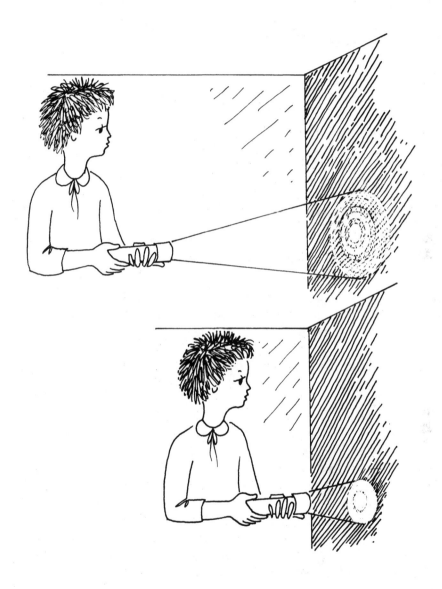

63. Brighter

Purpose To demonstrate how size affects a star's apparent brightness.

Materials *2 flashlights*
aluminum foil
pencil
2 sheets of blank paper

Procedure

- *Cover the lens end of one of the flashlights with a piece of aluminum foil.*
- *Make a hole in the center of the aluminum foil. Use the pencil to hollow this hole so that it is about as big around as your index finger.*
- *Lay the paper sheets 4 in. (10 cm) apart on a table.*
- *In a darkened room, hold one flashlight about 6 in. (15 cm) above each sheet of paper.*

Results The uncovered flashlight produces a larger, brighter circle of light.

Why? The larger the opening at the end of the flashlight, the brighter the beam of light on the paper sheet. A star's size, like the flashlight opening, affects the brightness of the star. The larger the star, the brighter the light seen on Earth. Stars have varying sizes. Some are smaller than the Earth. The Sun is considered a medium-sized star, with a diameter of 870,000 miles (1,392,000 km). Supergiant stars have diameters up to 1,000 times that of the Sun. The measure of a star's brightness as it is seen from the Earth is known as *magnitude*. A star's magnitude depends on three things—size, distance from the Earth, and temperature. Large, hot stars that are close to the Earth shine brightly in the night sky.

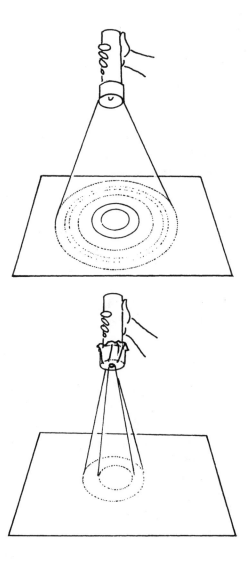

64. Daytime Stars

Purpose To demonstrate that the stars are always shining.

Materials *paper hole punch*
index card
1 white letter envelope
flashlight

Procedure

- *Cut 7 to 8 holes in the index card with the hole punch.*
- *Insert the index card in the envelope.*
- *In a well-lighted room, hold the envelope in front of you with the flashlight about 2 in. (5 cm) from the front of the envelope and over the index card.*
- *Move the flashlight behind the envelope.*
- *Hold the flashlight about 2 in. (5 cm) from the back of the envelope.*

Results The holes in the index card are not seen when the light shines on the front side of the envelope, but are easily seen when the light comes from behind the envelope and toward you.

Why? Light from the room passes through the holes in the card regardless of the position of the flashlight, but only when the surrounding area is darker than the light coming through the holes can they be seen. This is also true of stars. They shine during the daylight hours, but the sky is so bright from the Sun's light that the starlight just blends in. Stars are most visible on a moonless night in areas away from city lights.

140

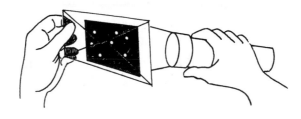

141

65. Streaks

Purpose To determine why stars appear to rotate.

Materials *ruler*
black construction paper
white chalk
pencil
masking tape
scissors

Procedure

- *Cut a circle with a 6-in. (15-cm) diameter from the black paper.*
- *Use chalk to randomly place 10 small dots on the black circle.*
- *Insert the point of the pencil through the center of the paper.*
- *Use tape to secure the pencil to the underside of the paper circle.*
- *Twirl the pencil back and forth between the palms of your hands.*

Results Rings of light appear on the spinning paper.

Why? Your mind retains the image of the chalk dots as the paper spins, causing the paper to appear to have rings on it. A similar picture is produced when astronomers expose photographic plates under starlight for several hours. The light from the stars continuously affects the exposed film, producing streaks as if the stars were moving in a circular path. The truth is that the stars are relatively stationary and the Earth is moving. The stars just appear to move around in the sky, but actually the film is moving with the Earth as it spins on its axis.

142

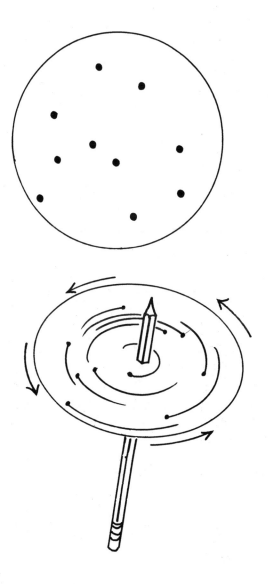

66. Box Planetarium

Purpose To demonstrate how planetariums produce images of the night sky.

Materials *shoe box*
black construction paper
cellophane tape
flashlight
straight pin
scissors

Procedure

- *Cut a square from the end of the shoe box.*
- *At the other end of the box, cut a circle just large enough to insert the end of the flashlight.*
- *Cover the square opening with a piece of black paper. Secure the paper to the box with tape.*
- *Use the pin to make 7 to 8 holes in the black paper.*
- *Point the shoebox toward a blank wall.*
- *In a darkened room, turn on the flashlight.*
- *Move back and forth from the wall to form clear images of small light spots on the wall. Make the holes in the black paper larger if the spots on the wall are too small.*

Results An enlarged pattern of the holes made in the paper are projected onto the wall.

Why? As light beams shine through the tiny holes, they spread outward producing larger circles of light on the wall. A planetarium presentation showing the entire night sky uses a round sphere with holes spaced in the positions of single stars and *constellations*. A constellation is a group of stars whose arrangement forms an imaginary figure. A bright light in the center of the sphere projects light spots on a curved ceiling representing the sky. As the ball rotates, different star groups are seen. Because of the Earth's revolution around the Sun, different stars are viewed in the sky at different times of the year.

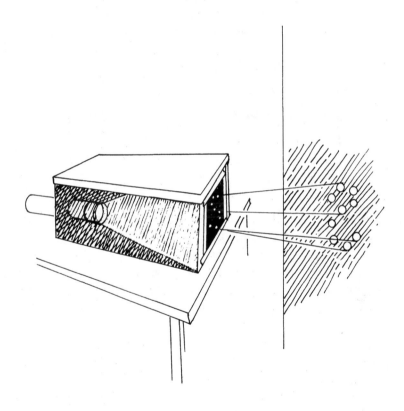

67. Hazy

Purpose To demonstrate why the Milky Way appears to be a hazy cloud.

Materials *paper hole punch*
black construction paper
white paper
glue
masking tape

Procedure

- *Use the hole punch to cut about 20 circles from the white paper.*
- *Glue the circles very close together in the center of the black sheet of paper.*
- *Tape the paper to a tree or any outside object.*
- *Stand near and look at the paper, then slowly back away until the separate circles can no longer be seen.*

Results The separate circles can be seen when standing near the paper, but at a distance, the circles blend together to form one large white shape.

Why? Due to the inability of our eye to distinguish discrete points of light that are too close together, the separate circles blend together as does the light from distant stars. Using binoculars or a telescope helps our eyes to see stars more clearly. The Milky Way galaxy is a group of stars and other celestial bodies, including our solar system, moving through the universe. Part of that galaxy appears as a milky haze in the night sky. This hazy light is actually light from billions of stars so far away that their light blurs. This haziness is partly due to the inability of our eyes to separate distant light sources, but great amounts of galactic dust also scatter and block the starlight from the Milky Way.

68. Unequal

Purpose To determine why variable stars pulsate.

Materials *round balloon, 9 in. (23 cm)*

Procedure
- *Partially inflate the balloon. Keep the end of the balloon in your mouth during the experiment.*
- *Use the pressure of your breath to keep the air from escaping.*
- *Force more air into the balloon.*
- *Allow some of the air to escape.*

Results The balloon increases and decreases in size.

Why? The balloon changes in size because the pressure inside the balloon changes, and the balloon stretches and shrinks as the air inside changes. *Cepheids* are variable stars that, like the balloon, change size depending on internal pressures. These stars, unlike others, are not at equilibrium, meaning that their gravity pulling inward does not equal the light and heat pressure pushing outward. As cepheids change size, they also change temperature and give off a different amount of light. When hottest, the star appears yellow and when cool, it looks orange. Cepheids are stars that have regular pulsations.

GRAVITY

149

69. Burn Out!

Purpose To determine the cause of "shooting stars."

Materials *block of wood*
nail
hammer

Procedure

■ *Partially hammer the nail into the wooden block.*
■ *Carefully touch the head of the nail with your fingers.*

Results The nail head is hot.

Why? The rubbing of two objects together causes friction. Friction between the hammer and nail produces heat as does the rubbing together of a meteor and air molecules in the Earth's atmosphere. *Meteoroids* are variable-sized pieces of materials floating through space. If the meteoroid gets close enough, Earth's gravity pulls it into the atmosphere. The friction of the fast-moving meteoroid against the air molecules causes the meteoroid to heat up and glow. This glowing mass is now called a *meteor.* Meteors usually burn up before reaching the Earth's surface. The flash of light as the glowing meteor burns is called a "shooting star." Showers of meteors occur each year around January 3, August 12, October 21, and December 14 because on these dates the Earth passes through the orbits of various comets. Matter in the comet's orbit is pulled into the Earth's atmosphere. If a meteor reaches the Earth's surface, it is called a *meteorite.* Most meteorites are as small as dust particles or sand grains, but larger pieces have struck the Earth.

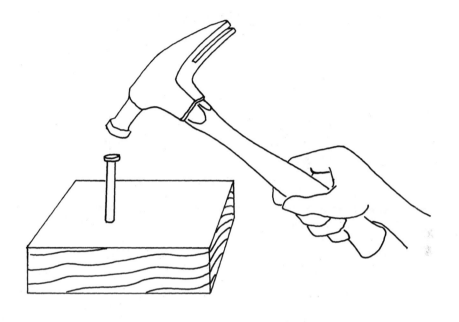

70. Silhouette

Purpose To simulate an absorption nebula.

Materials *table lamp*
1 sheet of typing paper
pencil

Procedure
Note: Perform this experiment in a darkened room.
- *Turn the table lamp on.*
- *Hold the sheet of paper about 1 yd. (1 m) in front of the lamp.*
- *Place the pencil about 2 in. (5 cm) from the paper on the side facing the lamp.*
- *Look at the paper facing you.*

Results A silhouette of the pencil forms on the paper.

Why? A *nebula* is a vast cloud of dust and gas in space. There are three classes of nebulae—absorption nebulae that block light, emission nebulae that glow, and reflection nebulae that reflect light from other objects.

The silhouette of the pencil simulates an absorption nebula, which blocks the light coming from behind it and appears as a dark silhouette. The shapes of these clouds in the heavens are due to the concentration of the particles making up the nebula that blocks the light of distant stars.

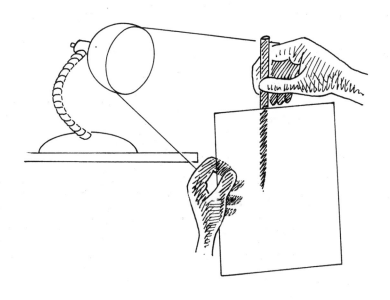

71. Spirals

Purpose To demonstrate the movement of a spiral galaxy.

Materials *1 sheet of notebook paper*
paper hole punch
jar, 1 qt. (1 liter)
pencil
water

Procedure
- *Fill the jar about three-fourths full with water.*
- *Cut about 20 circles from the paper with the hole punch.*
- *Sprinkle the paper circles on the surface of the water.*
- *Quickly stir the water in a circular motion with a pencil.*
- *View the water from the top and sides after you stop stirring.*

Results The paper circles swirl around, forming a spiral shape in the center.

Why? The spinning paper only simulates the spiral movement and concentration of material of a star-studded *spiral galaxy*. Galaxies are thicker in the center; they actually bulge. The Milky Way galaxy is a spiral galaxy. It takes the Milky Way 250 million years to make one complete turn, but much space is covered during this rotation by the more than 200 billion stars. Our solar system is just a small part of this large spiraling mass that is 100,000 light years from edge to edge. A light year is a measure of distance and not time. One light year means that it takes light, traveling at a speed of 186,000 miles (300,000 km) per second, one entire year to travel the distance.

154

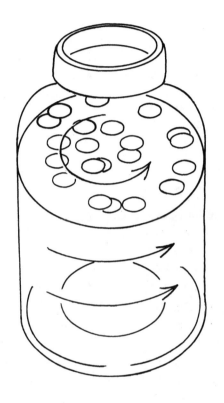

72. Star Chart

Purpose To record the position of the Big Dipper and Polaris.

Materials *white poster paper*
string
large nail
marker
helper

Procedure

- *Cut a string 12 in. (30 cm) longer than your height.*
- *Tie one end of the string to a nail.*
- *On a clear, moonless night, lay a sheet of white poster paper on the ground.*
- *Stand on the edge of the paper and point to a star in the Big Dipper constellation while holding the free end of the string, allowing the nail to hang freely.*
- *Ask a helper to mark a spot on the paper under the hanging nail.*
- *Point to each of the stars in the Big Dipper as your helper marks their position on the paper.*
- *Find and mark the position of the North Star by drawing a straight line from the first star in the bowl of the dipper to the star in the handle of ursa minor, the Little Dipper constellation.*

Results The position of part of the ursa major *constellation* called the Big Dipper is drawn on the paper and Polaris, the North Star, is plotted on the star chart.

Why? As your finger moves from one star to the next, the free hanging nail moves to a new position, thus plotting the position of the stars. Polaris, the star that the Earth's imaginary axis points to, is also called the North Star. This star can be found by allowing the first star in the bowl of the Big Dipper to be the pointer star.

POLARIS

73. Twinkling Star

Purpose To determine why stars twinkle.

Materials *flashlight*
aluminum foil
glass bowl, 2 qt. (2 liter)
pencil

Procedure

- *Cut a piece of aluminum foil large enough to fit under the bowl. Wrinkle this piece of foil with your hands.*
- *Fill the bowl half full with water and place it on top of the wrinkled piece of aluminum foil.*
- *In a darkened room, hold the flashlight about 12 in. (30 cm) from the top of the bowl.*
- *Observe the foil and take note of how it appears when viewed through undisturbed water.*
- *Continue to shine the light through the water as you gently tap the surface of the water with a pencil.*
- *Observe the foil as it appears when viewed through moving water.*

Results The moving water causes the light reflecting from the aluminum foil to blur.

Why? Light travels in a straight line, and the waves on the water's surface cause the light rays to leave in different directions. This change in the direction of light rays is called *refraction.* Other light sources, such as stars, behave in the same manner when the light passes through moving material. A star appears to twinkle when viewed from the Earth because the star's light passes through layers of moving air before reaching the viewer's eyes. The light is bent this way and that as it moves through whirling packets of air in the Earth's atmosphere. The scientific term for twinkling is *scintillation.* Stars do not scintillate (twinkle) when viewed from a spacecraft above the Earth's atmosphere because there is not enough material in space to refract the star's light.

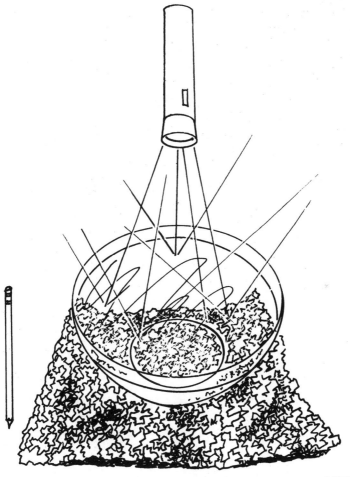

VI
Space Instruments

74. Up or Down?

Purpose To demonstrate how light travels through the lens of a refractive telescope.

Materials *goose-neck desk lamp*
magnifying lens
dark construction paper, 1 sheet
scissors
masking tape

Procedure

- *Cut a paper circle from the dark paper to fit the opening of the lamp.*
- *Cut an arrow design in the center of the paper circle.*
- *Tape the circle over the lamp.*
  Caution: Be sure that the paper does not rest on the lightbulb. The bulb will get hot.
- *Place the lamp about 6 ft. (2 m) from a wall.*
- *Darken the room with the exception of the lamp.*
- *Hold the magnifying lens about 12 in. (30 cm) from the lamp.*
- *Move the magnifying lens back and forth from the lamp until a clear image is projected on the wall.*

Results The image produced on the wall is turned upside down.

Why? Light travels in a straight line, but when it hits the lens, it changes direction, causing the image to be upside down. Refractive telescopes have lenses similar to the one used in this experiment, and so stars viewed through a refractive telescope appear upside down.

162

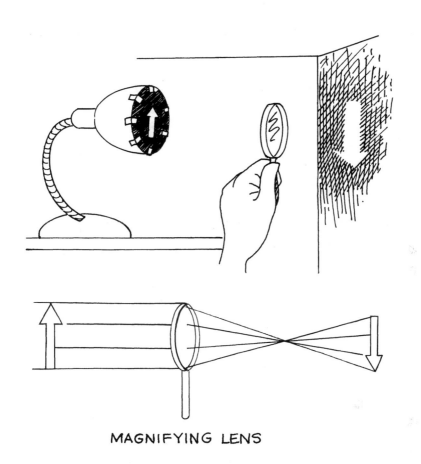

MAGNIFYING LENS

163

75. Sharp

Purpose To demonstrate how size affects telescope images.

Materials *typing paper, 3 sheets*
cellophane tape
goose-neck desk lamp
scissors

Procedure

■ *Roll two sheets of paper into cones, making one cone much wider than the other.*

■ *Use the scissors to cut off the tip of the cones to make an equal-sized opening in each cone.*

■ *Place the last sheet of paper on the table near the lamp.*

■ *Hold one cone at a time under the lamp. The end of each cone must be the same height from the table.*

■ *Move each cone to the right until the spot of light formed by the cone is not seen.*

■ *Observe the light projected onto the paper by each cone.*

Results The larger cone produces a brighter spot of light on the paper and continues to produce a light spot farther from the lamp.

Why? The larger cone collects more light and funnels it down to the paper. The telescopes used to study the stars have a very large end directed toward the sky and behave in the same way as the cone. The over-sized end of the telescope collects large quantities of light, resulting in brighter images of the stars. Because large telescopes collect more light, they can detect the presence of dimmer stars.

164

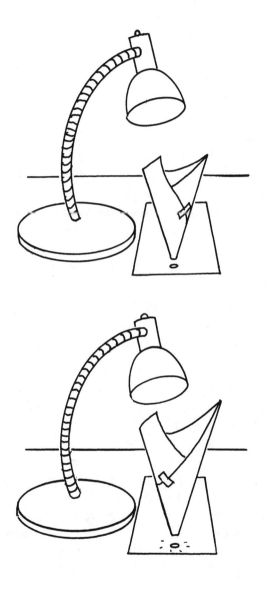

76. Simple

Purpose To demonstrate how a refracting telescope works.

Materials *sheet of notebook paper*
2 magnifying lenses

Procedure

- *In a darkened room, close one eye and look at an open window through one of the magnifying lenses.*
- *Move the lens back and forth slowly until the objects outside the window are clearly in focus.*
- *Without moving the lens, place a sheet of paper between you and the lens.*
- *Move the paper back and forth until a clear image appears on the sheet.*
- *Replace the paper with the second lens.*
- *Move the second lens back and forth to find the position where the image looks clear when looking through both lenses.*

Results A small, inverted image of the objects outside the window is projected onto the paper. The image seen through both lenses is upside down and larger than when seen through one lens.

Why? The furthermost lens is called the objective lens. It collects light from the distant objects and brings it into focus. At the focal point, an image, or picture, of the object exists and can be projected onto a screen. The second lens, called the eyepiece lens, collects light from the image and brings an enlarged, inverted image into focus in front of your eyes.

166

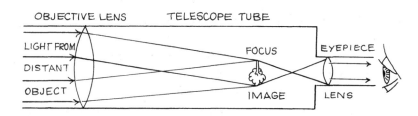

OBJECTIVE LENS   TELESCOPE TUBE

LIGHT FROM   FOCUS   EYEPIECE

DISTANT

OBJECT   IMAGE   LENS

77. Reflector

Purpose To demonstrate how a reflective telescope works.

Materials *goose-neck desk lamp*
shaving mirror
magnifying lens
black construction paper
scissors
masking tape

Procedure

■ *Cut a circle from the black paper large enough to cover the opening of the desk lamp.*

■ *Cut out an arrow shape in the center of the paper.*

■ *Cover the light with the paper circle and secure it with tape.*
Caution: *Be sure that the paper does not rest on the lightbulb. The bulb will get hot.*

■ *Place the mirror about 20 in. (50 cm) from the lamp. Turn the side of the mirror that gives the largest image toward the lamp.*

■ *Move the mirror so that a clear image of the arrow is projected onto a wall.*

■ *Look at the image of the arrow through a magnifying lens.*

Results An enlarged and inverted image of the arrow is seen.

Why? Light from the mirror is collected by the shaving mirror, a concave mirror, which produces an inverted image.

The wall acts as a flat mirror that reflects the image to the magnifying lens, the eyepiece in the telescope. The lens magnifies the image.

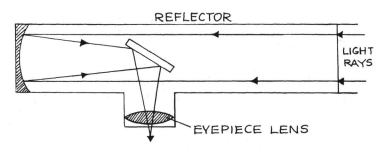

REFLECTOR

LIGHT RAYS

EYEPIECE LENS

78. Space Balance

Purpose To determine how mass can be measured in space.

Materials *hacksaw blade, 10 in. (25.5 cm)*
4 coins, any size
masking tape

Procedure
Caution: Have an adult cover the teeth of the blade with a strip of masking tape.

- *Tape the blade to the edge of a table.*
- *Pull the free end of the blade back and release it.*
- *Observe the speed at which the blade moves.*
- *Use tape to attach two coins to the end of the blade, one on each side.*
- *Pull the blade back as before and release it.*
- *Attach two more coins to the blade and swing the blade as before.*

Results As more coins are added, the speed of the swinging blade decreases.

Why? The swinging blade is called an *inertia balance.* Because the back-and-forth swing of the blade is the same in and out of a gravity field, the balance can be used as a measuring tool in space. *Inertia* is that property of matter by which it resists any sudden change in its state of motion or rest. As the mass of an object increases, the object's inertia increases. Therefore, it is more difficult to move a large mass. You applied the same amount of energy to each swing, but as the mass increased, it took more energy to move it. The number of swings for a specific mass could be determined, and by counting the number of swings, the mass of an object can be calculated.

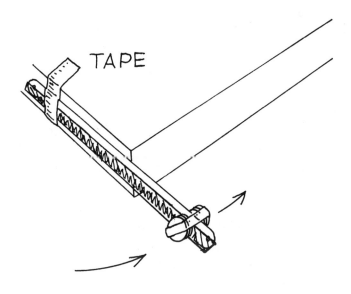

TAPE

79. Retroreflector

Purpose To determine how to measure the distance to the Moon.

Materials *flashlight*
masking tape
sheet of notebook paper
2 flat mirrors

Procedure

■ *The experiment should be performed in a room that can be darkened.*

■ *Tape the edge of the mirrors together so that they open and close like a book.*

■ *Stand the mirrors on a table.*

■ *Tape the paper to the front of your shirt to form a screen.*

■ *Place the flashlight on the table so that the light strikes one of the mirrors at an angle.*

■ *Change the angle of the second mirror to find a position that reflects the light back to the screen on your shirt.*

Results A ring of light appeared on the paper screen.

Why? The light was reflected from one mirror to another before bouncing back to the paper screen. The *retroreflector* left on the Moon was a set of mirrors similar to the ones in this experiment. The amount of time it took for a laser beam from Earth to reflect off the two and a half feet square retroreflector was measured and the distance from the Earth to the Moon calculated.

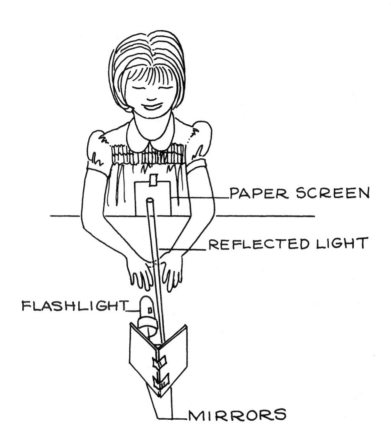

PAPER SCREEN

REFLECTED LIGHT

FLASHLIGHT

MIRRORS

173

80. Pinhole Camera

Purpose To demonstrate that light travels in a straight line.

Materials *coffee can, 1 lb. (454 grams)*
wax paper
black construction paper
scissors
masking tape
rubber band
hammer
nail

Procedure

- *Have an adult punch a small hole in the center of the can's closed end with the hammer and nail.*
- *Cover the open end of the can with wax paper. Secure the paper with a rubber band.*
- *Cut a 14-in. (35-cm) square from the construction paper.*
- *Wrap the black paper around the circumference of the coffee can like a sleeve. Secure with tape.*
- *Leave about 10 in. (25 cm) of the black paper extending from the end of the can with the wax paper–covered end in the middle and the end with the nail hole farthest away.*
- *Darken a room and point the tiny hole in the can toward a window.*
- *Hold the black paper cylinder up to your eyes.*

Results Images formed on the wax paper are upside down and backwards and in color.

174

Why? Light traveling at an angle plus the ray coming straight at the opening enter the tiny hole in the can. Since light always travels in a straight line, the reflected light from the top of the object looked at (the car in the diagram) hits the bottom of the paper screen, and other parts of the image do the same. This causes the object to appear upside down and backwards on the screen. Refer to Experiment 43 for instructions on using a small hole in a card to project an inverted image of the Sun onto a paper screen.

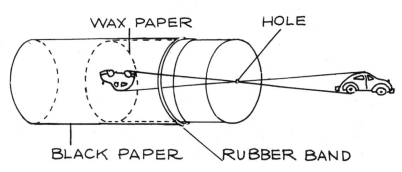

WAX PAPER   HOLE

BLACK PAPER   RUBBER BAND

81. How High?

Purpose To determine how distance can be compared using an astrolabe.

Materials *drinking straw*
protractor
masking tape
string
heavy bolt
ruler
helper

Procedure

■ *Cut a 12-in. (30-cm) piece of string.*
■ *Tie one end of the string to the center of the protractor and attach the bolt to the other end of the string.*
■ *Tape the straw along the top edge of the protractor.*
■ *Look through the straw (keeping one eye closed) at the tops of distant objects and have your helper determine the angle of the hanging string.*

Results The angle increases as the height of the objects increases.

Why? To see the tops of the distant objects, the protractor had to be elevated. The hanging string remains perpendicular to the ground because gravity continues to pull it toward the center of the Earth. As the protractor turns, the string has a different angle in relation to the straw. This instrument is called an *astrolabe* and can be used to compare the distances between stars, since the distance increases as the angle increases.

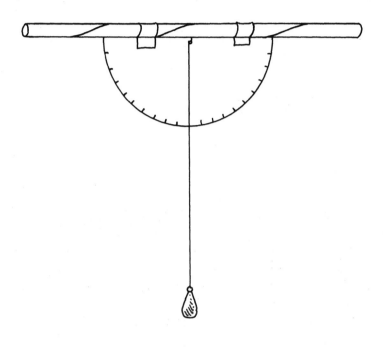

177

82. Spectroscope

Purpose To demonstrate how star composition can be determined.

Materials *record*
sheet of dark-colored construction paper
scissors
ruler

Procedure

- *Fold the paper in half.*
- *Cut a 2-in. (10-cm) slit in the center of the paper's fold.*
- *Place the record inside the folded paper with its edge at the slit.*
- *Hold the edge of the record in front of your right eye.*
- *Point the slit in the paper at different light sources such as a lighted window, tungsten bulbs, mercury vapor street lights, and neon signs.*
Caution: Do not look directly at the Sun.
- *The light should barely graze the grooves on the record.*
- *Close your left eye and look at the grooves with your right eye.*
- *Slightly tilt the record until colors appear on the record's surface.*

Results Bands of color are seen on the record. The tungsten bulb and light from the window produce a full spectrum in this order: red, orange, yellow, green, blue, and violet. The mercury and neon lights produce only a portion of the spectrum colors.

178

Why? The record behaves like a *spectroscope,* an instrument that breaks light into its individual colors. The light from the different sources does not have *all* of the colors of the spectrum—red, orange, yellow, green, blue, indigo and violet—as does solar light. The atoms on the Sun and in the different light bulbs and tubes used in this experiment all give off light when heated or placed in the path of charged particles such as an electric current. These atoms become excited when heated or hit by charged particles and release visible light. Each type of atom emits a specific color. Astronomers can study the colors emitted by a star and determine the type of atoms that make up the glowing celestial body.

83. Light Meter

Purpose To demonstrate how to measure the brightness of light.

Materials *yardstick (meter stick)*
small box such as a shoe box
aluminum foil
wax paper
scissors
cellophane tape
flashlight

Procedure

■ *Cut a large window in both ends of the box and two large windows in one side of the box.*

■ *Cover the openings with four layers of wax paper. Secure the paper with tape.*

■ *Fold a piece of aluminum so that it hangs in the center of the inside of the box, dividing the box. Secure the foil with tape.*

■ *Put the lid on.*

■ *In a darkened room, set the box on the floor and place the flashlight about 2 yd. (2 m) from the end of the box.*

■ *Observe the side windows.*

■ *Move the flashlight to 1 yd. (1 m) then 1/2 yd. (1/2 m) from the box's end.*

Results The side facing the light gets brighter as the light nears the box.

Why? The aluminum foil reflects the light and the wax paper scatters it, causing the side facing the flashlight to be

180

brighter. The brightness increases as the light source nears the box. The box is an example of a *photometer,* an instrument used to measure the brightness of a light. A more sensitive photoelectric meter can be used to measure the brightness of light from stars. A star closer to the Earth is much brighter than one of equal energy that is farther away.

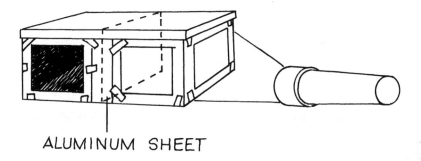

ALUMINUM SHEET

84. Collector

Purpose To demonstrate the effect of metal on energy waves.

Materials *television with a remote control*
aluminum foil
masking tape

Procedure

- *Use the remote control to change the channels on the television.*
- *Fold a 12-in. (30-cm) square piece of aluminum foil in half and cover the receiving eye on the television. Attach the foil with tape.*
- *Try to change the channels using the remote control.*

Results The remote control does not work when the aluminum foil is in front of the receiving eye on the television.

Why? The Sun and other stars are constantly emitting energy in the form of waves. Radio waves, like visible light, infrared waves, and others, are examples of these energy waves. These radio waves coming from celestial bodies provides a way to study the invisible, most distant parts of our universe. In this experiment, aluminum, a very lightweight, nonmagnetic metal, is used to block the infrared energy signals coming from the remote control devices. This metal also blocks radio waves and is used in making the large bowl-shaped radio telescopes to reflect radio waves coming from distant stars. These reflected waves are directed toward a receiver that transmits them to a computer, and finally a recorded message is printed. The largest radio telescope is in Arecibo, Puerto Rico, and is the size of 13 football fields.

182

RECEIVER   COMPUTER   RECORDER

85. Around the World

Purpose To demonstrate how a satellite's position affects the direction of its signal.

Materials *coffee can, 1 lb.*
black construction paper
cellophane tape
flashlight
flat mirror
yardstick (meter stick)
modeling clay
scissors

Procedure
Note: Perform this experiment in a room that can be darkened.
- *Cover the outside of the can with construction paper.*
- *Tape a paper flap about 4 in. (10 cm) square to one side of the can.*
- *Place the yardstick in front of the can.*
- *Use the clay to make a stand for the mirror.*
- *Set the mirror on top of the yardstick near the can.*
- *Darken the room.*
- *Turn the light on and place it at a slight angle to the side of the can opposite the paper flap.*
- *Move the mirror away from the can until light from the flashlight is projected onto the paper flap.*

Results The position of the mirror changes the direction of the light path.

184

Why? Light leaves the flashlight in a straight line. The mirror must be far enough from the can to reflect the light to the paper flap. The movement of the light from one side of the can to the opposite side is similar to the transmission of radio waves around the Earth via satellites. A communications satellite in orbit above the Earth's equator, 22,300 miles (36,000 km) in space, is used to transmit radio signals from one place on the Earth to a receiver on the opposite side of the Earth. Closer satellites could not send a reflected radio wave in a straight line from one side of the curved Earth to the other. More than 120 communications satellites circle the Earth's equator. There is no point on the Earth's surface that cannot communicate with the rest of the world via satellite. Communications satellites can simultaneously relay two dozen television programs, thousands of telephone calls, and millions of bits of electronic data. The reason why communication satellites are in orbit 22,300 miles (36,000 km) above the Earth is that at this distance the satellite is in a *geosynchronous* orbit. Geosynchronous means that the satellite will always be in the same position over the Earth even though the Earth rotates around its axis and the satellite spins around the Earth.

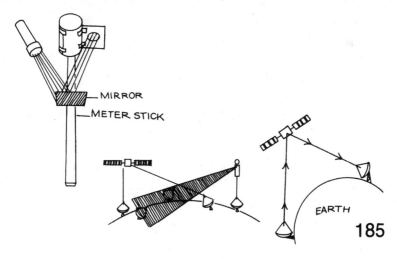

MIRROR

METER STICK

EARTH

185

86. Focus

Purpose To determine why radio wave receivers are curved.

Materials *jar, 1 qt. (1 liter)*
aluminum foil
flashlight
sheet of black construction paper
index card
modeling clay
scissors

Procedure

- *Cut four 1 in. (2.5 cm) high slits about 1/4 in. (.5 cm) wide and 1/4 in. (.5 cm) apart in the index card.*
- *Use clay to stand the card in the center of the black paper.*
- *Continue to fold a 12-in. (30-cm) square piece of aluminum foil to form a strip about 6 in. × 1 in. (15 cm × 2.5 cm).*
- *Mold the aluminum strip around the side of the jar to form a curved metal mirror.*
- *Place the flashlight on one side of the card and the curved aluminum mirror on the opposite side.*
- *Use clay to raise the back of the flashlight.*
- *In a darkened room, move the flashlight back and forth from the card until straight lines of light pass through the slits in the card.*
- *Move the aluminum back and forth until the clearest image is seen.*

Results The reflected lines from the aluminum mirror leave the surface of the metal at an angle and meet at one point in front of the mirror.

186

Why? Light is reflected from the concave (inward-curved) mirror to a central focal point. Radio waves, like the light, can be reflected from concave surfaces to a point where a type of microphone is positioned to send the concentrated waves on to another receiver. Large bowl-shaped dishes are used to receive radio waves from distant stars just as home satellite dishes collect television transmissions.

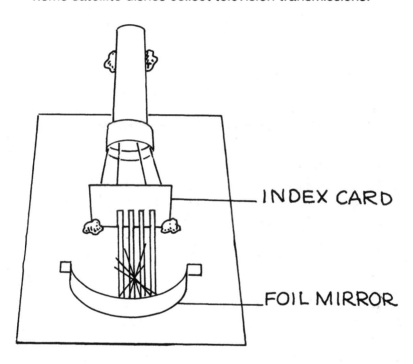

INDEX CARD

FOIL MIRROR

187

87. Bouncer

Purpose To demonstrate how communication satellites work.

Materials *flashlight*
flat mirror
helper
modeling clay

Procedure

- *Use the clay to stand the mirror on a table positioned near an open door.*
- *Have a person stand in the next room so that he or she can see the mirror, but not see you.*
- *Shine the light on the surface of the mirror.*
- *You and your helper need to find a position that allows the light to reflect from the mirror so that your helper sees the light, but does not see you.*

Results The light beam is sent from one room and seen by a person in another room.

Why? The shiny surface of the mirror reflects the light. Radio waves, like the light, can be reflected from smooth surfaces and directed to receivers at different places around the world. A signal sent to an orbiting satellite is bounced back at an angle to a receiver many miles away from the sender.

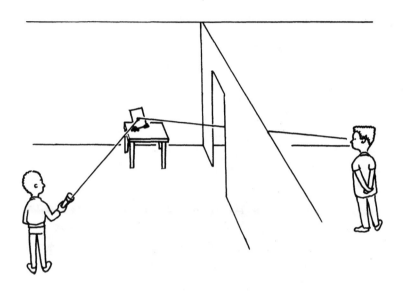

88. Blending

Purpose To demonstrate the resolution of a lens.

Materials *flashlight*
black construction paper
straight pin
scissors
ruler
masking tape
pencil

Procedure

- *Cut a circle of paper to fit over the end of the flashlight.*
- *Secure the paper to the flashlight end with tape.*
- *Use the pin to make two holes in the center of the paper circle about the width of the pencil lead apart.*
- *Place the flashlight on a table.*
- *Stand near the flashlight, facing the two spots of light emitted.*
- *Slowly walk backwards until the spots look like one dot.*

Results The two holes appear as one beam of light from a distance.

Why? *Resolution* measures the ability to see details. The resolving power of a telescope lens indicates the lens's ability to distinguish between the images of two points. The greater the resolution, the better one can see the object studied. The resolving power of a lens increases with the diameter of the lens. Atmospheric conditions also affect resolving power.

This is true with your own eyes as well as with telescopes. Since clouds and pollution reduce the resolution of a telescope, placing a telescope in an orbit above the Earth's atmosphere frees it from this problem. The first orbiting telescope, the Hubble telescope, was launched April 24, 1990, and placed in an orbit about 375 miles (600 km) above the Earth's surface. Without interference from the Earth's atmosphere, the Hubble's resolution power is 10 to 12 times greater than a telescope of comparable size on the Earth's surface.

PINHOLES

VII

Space and Space Travel

89. Blast Off

Purpose To demonstrate how rockets move in space.

Materials *balloon, 9 in. (23 cm)*

Procedure
- *Inflate the balloon and hold the mouth of the balloon shut between your fingers.*
- *Release the balloon and allow it to move freely.*

Results The balloon moves around the room as it deflates.

Why? When the inflated balloon is closed, the air inside pushes equally in all directions. As the air leaves the balloon, the opening moves back and forth, acting like a rudder directing the balloon in its irregular path through the air. The balloon, like a rocket, moves because of *Newton's Third Law of Motion* which states that for every action there is an equal and opposite reaction. In the case of the balloon, the rubber pushes on the air inside (action), forcing it out the opening. The air pushes on the balloon (reaction). The reaction force of the air pushes the balloon in the opposite direction of the action force. Like the balloon, spacecraft are able to move forward due to action-reaction forces. The engines of a rocket produce gases that are pushed out the exhaust (action), and the gas applies a force on the rocket (reaction). The reaction force pushes against the rocket, causing it to lift up.

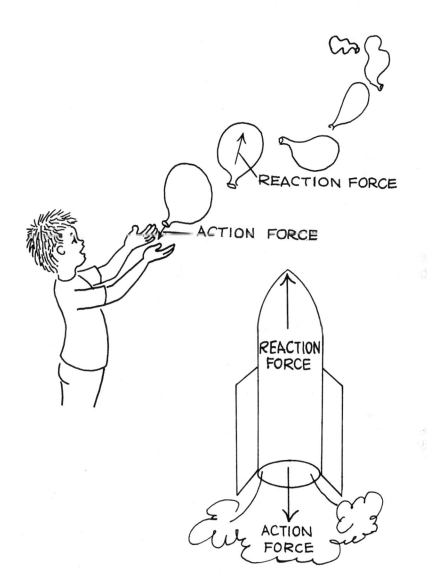

REACTION FORCE

ACTION FORCE

REACTION FORCE

ACTION FORCE

195

90. Staging

Purpose To demonstrate rocket staging.

Materials *balloon, 9 in. (23 cm), round*
long balloon, 18 in. (45 cm)
paper cup, 5 oz. (150 ml)
scissors

Procedure
- *Cut the bottom from the paper cup.*
- *Partially inflate the long balloon and pull the open end of the balloon through the top and out the bottom of the cup.*
- *Fold the top of the balloon over the edge of the cup to keep the air from escaping as you place the round balloon inside the cup and inflate it.*
- *Release the mouth of the round balloon.*

Results The attached balloons move forward quickly as the round balloon deflates. The cup falls away and the final balloon speeds forward as it deflates.

Why? The set of balloons represents a three-stage rocket. Great amounts of fuel are needed to lift and move heavy spacecraft. Each stage of the rocket system has its own set of engines and fuel supply. As each stage uses up its fuel, it drops away making the rocket system lighter. Each stage lifts the craft until finally the payload is put into orbit or achieves a fast enough speed to leave the Earth's atmosphere for a trip into space.

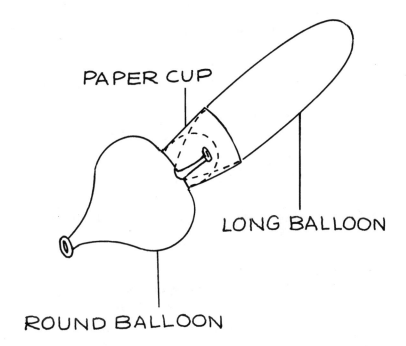

PAPER CUP

LONG BALLOON

ROUND BALLOON

91. Fake

Purpose To demonstrate how artificial gravity can be produced.

Materials *record player*
round cake pan
4 marbles
2 sheets of construction paper —any color
scissors
modeling clay

Procedure

- *Cut a circle from one sheet of paper to fit inside the pan.*
- *Cover the turntable with a sheet of paper to protect it.*
- *Center the pan on the turntable and use three lumps of clay to raise the pan above the turntable's spindle.*
- *Place the marbles in the center of the pan.*
- *Turn the record player to its highest speed for 30 seconds, then turn it off.*

Results As the pan starts to spin, the marbles move forward until they hit the side of the pan.

Why? The movement of the pan starts the marbles moving. They continue to move in a straight line until the side of the pan stops them. The marbles press against the pan's side as long as the pan turns. In space, a turning space station would cause unattached objects inside to be pressed against the walls of the station just as the marbles press against the turning pan. A spinning space station must provide artificial gravity to allow astronauts to walk around and so that dropped objects would fall "down," "down" being toward the outside rim of the turning craft. The most likely shape for this spinning space station would be a large wheel.

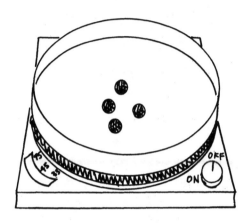

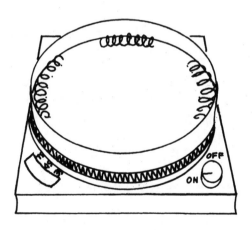

92. Flash!

Purpose To determine how crystal light might benefit space travel.

Materials *wintergreen candy*
hammer
wooden block
plastic sandwich bag

Procedure
Note: This experiment must be performed in a dark room. A closed closet works well.

- *Place one wintergreen candy in the plastic bag.*
- *Place the bag on the wooden block.*
- *Position the hammer above the candy.*
- *Look directly at the candy piece as you smash it with the hammer.*

Results A quick bluish-green flash of light is given off at the moment the candy crushes.

Why? Crystals broken by pressure give off light. This light is an example of *triboluminescence*. Crystals such as sugar and quartz give off light flashes when crushed. Crystals that give off light under pressure could possibly be used by engineers in designing the outer shield of space vehicles. It is possible that instruments on Earth could detect crystal light flashes that would indicate trouble spots.

93. Darkness

Purpose To demonstrate why space is dark.

Materials *flashlight*

Procedure
- *Place the flashlight on the edge of a table.*
- *Darken the room leaving only the flashlight on.*
- *Look at the beam of light leaving the flashlight and try to follow it across the room.*
- *Hold your hand about 12 in. (30 cm) from the end of the flashlight.*

Results A circular light pattern forms on your hand, but little or no light is seen between the flashlight and your hand.

Why? Your hand reflected the light to your eyes, making the beam visible. Space is dark even though the Sun's light continuously passes through it because there is nothing to reflect the light to your eyes. Light is seen only when it is reflected from an object to your eyes.

203

94. Escape

Purpose To demonstrate escape velocity.

Materials *magnet, any size or shape*
steel air-gun shot, BBs
large plastic lid
stiff paper
scissors
modeling clay
cellophane tape

Procedure

■ *Cut a 12 in. × 4 in. (30 cm × 10 cm) strip from the stiff paper.*

■ *Fold the paper to form an M-shape.*

■ *Place the magnet against the inside edge of the plastic lid.*

■ *Spread the M-shaped paper so that the center trough is widened.*

■ *Attach the end of the trough to the edge of the magnet with a small piece of tape.*

■ *Use the clay to slightly elevate the unattached end of the paper trough.*

■ *Place one BB at the top of the trough and allow it to roll toward the magnet.*

■ *Raise the trough and allow another BB to roll down.*

■ *Continue to raise the trough until a rolling BB does not stick to the magnet.*

Results The BBs roll down the trough and stick to the magnet when the trough is slightly raised. At a higher elevation, the BBs slow down when they touch the magnet, but roll past into the plastic lid.

Why? The rolling balls have *momentum* because they are moving and have mass. Momentum is defined as the mass of an object times its velocity. Raising the trough increases the velocity of the balls, which in turn increase their momentum. With the greater momentum, it becomes harder for the magnet to stop them. A velocity is eventually reached that produces a momentum large enough to overcome the pull of the magnet. The velocity of the BBs can be compared to the escape velocity of rockets leaving the Earth's atmosphere. The BBs are escaping the magnetic pull of the magnet and the rocket is escaping the pull of gravity toward the Earth. Escape velocity is about 25,000 miles/hr (40,000 km/hr).

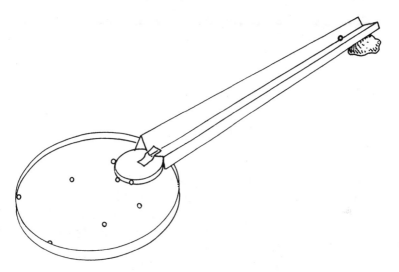

95. Spheres

Purpose To demonstrate the effect of forces on the shape of drops of liquid in space.

Materials *liquid cooking oil*
1 clear drinking glass
eye dropper
rubbing alcohol

Procedure
- *Fill the glass one-half full with water.*
- *Tilt the glass and very slowly fill the glass with alcohol by pouring the alcohol down the inside of the glass. This will keep it from mixing with the water.*
- *Add 4 to 5 drops of oil to the glass.*
- *Observe the position of the oil and its shape.*

Results Round spheres of oil float between the alcohol and water layer.

Why? Drops of liquid form a spherical shape because of *surface tension* (the tendency of the surface of a liquid to contract). This contraction is due to *cohesive forces,* the attraction between like particles. The oil drops stay suspended between the layers of water and alcohol because the oil does not dissolve in either liquid. The oil is heavier than the alcohol but lighter than the water, and thus it falls through the alcohol and floats on the surface of the water. Beneath the surface of the liquids, every particle of each oil drop is attracted equally in all directions by neighboring particles. This produces the same results as releasing a drop of liquid in space. In both situations, the cohesive forces pull the liquid into a spherical shape. The shape would be perfectly spherical under the surface of a liquid if the neighboring particles pulled exactly equally in all directions. Pulling equally in all directions gives the same result as not pulling at all. Space can provide an environment with a very small gravitational pull that would allow the cohesive forces in a released drop of liquid to pull it into a near-perfect spherical shape.

96. Stop!

Purpose To demonstrate how gravity affects inertia.

Materials *cereal (your choice)*
milk
bowl
spoon

Procedure

- *Prepare your favorite cereal.*
- *Eat a spoonful of cereal.*
- *Raise a second spoonful of cereal to your mouth, but stop before putting the food in your mouth.*
- *Observe the position of the spoon and its contents.*

Results When the spoon is stopped, the food stays in the spoon.

Why? This experiment does not present any mystifying results. Of course the food stays in the spoon, but is that always true? No! If you were eating in space and stopped the spoon before it reached your mouth, you would receive a face full of food. Gravity is pulling down with enough force to keep the food from moving forward when the spoon stops moving. *Inertia* means that an object in motion continues to move until stopped by some force. In space, the inertia of the food would keep it moving after the spoon had been stopped.

97. Free Fall

Purpose To demonstrate apparent weightlessness.

Materials plastic drinking glass
string
ruler
scissors
masking tape
modeling clay
helper

Procedure

- Cut a 24-in. (60-cm) length of string.
- Use tape to attach the ends of the string to the top of the cup, one on each side.
- Tie a 6-in. (15-cm) piece of string in the center of the longer string.
- Mold a grape-sized piece of clay around the end of the short string.
- Ask a helper to hold the top of the short string and raise the cup and clay ball as high as possible, and then release them.
- While sitting in a chair, observe the position of the ball and cup as they fall.

Results The clay ball hangs above the cup until the cup is stopped, and then the clay falls into the cup.

Why? The clay and the cup are falling at the same speed. The cup continues to fall away from the clay ball until the cup is stopped. Falling objects experience an apparent weightlessness, a feeling of zero gravity. This is because only gases in the environment through which they are falling press against the object. Astronauts in spacecraft orbiting the Earth experience apparent weightlessness as does any falling object, because the craft and contents are constantly falling around the Earth. Roller coaster rides simulate a zero gravity feeling as the cars move down steep inclines. Objects are never weightless because there is always a pull of gravity from some object. It is true that at a distance greater than 187,500 miles (300,000 km) from the Earth's surface spacecraft are not pulled toward the Earth, but they are pulled on by the gravity of other celestial bodies such as the Moon or planets.

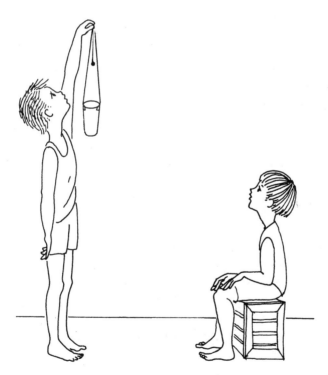

98. Protector

Purpose To determine how the materials in space suits help to regulate temperature.

Materials 2 thermometers
2 drinking glasses large enough to hold a thermometer
aluminum foil
rubber glove
desk lamp
cotton handkerchief

Procedure

■ Line the inside of one glass with the rubber glove, and cover the outside of the glass with aluminum foil.

■ Line the inside of the second glass with the handkerchief.

■ Place a thermometer in each glass.

■ Set both glasses about 12 in. (30 cm) from the lamp.

■ Observe the temperature on both thermometers after 5 minutes.

Results The temperature is higher in the glass lined with the handkerchief.

Why? Materials that help in preventing temperature changes are called *insulators*. The rubber glove is a better insulating material than the thin cotton handkerchief, and the aluminum foil helped to keep the glass cooler inside by reflecting the light away from the glass. An astronaut's space suit must keep a constant temperature, and one way is to decrease the amount of heat transferred to the body from the Sun. Layers of insulating material, such as rubber and nylon, are used to make the suits, and an outer coating of aluminum is added to reflect the Sun's rays. The materials in the space suit help to maintain a constant temperature environment for the person inside.

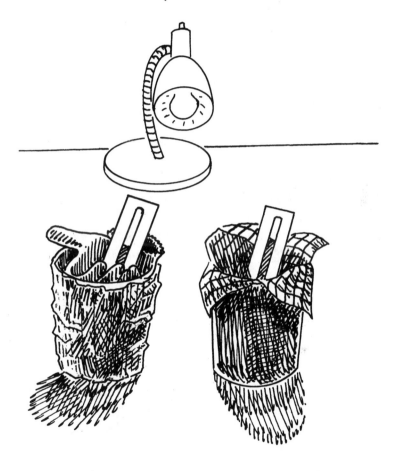

99. Space Suit

Purpose To demonstrate how space suits affect an astronaut's blood.

Materials *sealed bottle of cola*
clear drinking glass

Procedure
- *Observe the liquid in the sealed bottle of cola for 1 minute.*
- *Open the bottle of cola.*
- *Fill the glass with cola.*
- *Taste the cola in the glass.*
- *Observe the liquid in the glass for 1 minute.*
- *Allow the glass to stand undisturbed for 5 minutes.*
- *Taste the cola in the glass.*
  Note: *Never taste anything in a laboratory setting unless you are sure that there are no harmful chemicals or materials.*

Results Gas bubbles rise to the surface of the liquid in the open glass container, but no bubbles are seen in the sealed bottle. The cola has a tart, acid taste when first tasted, but after standing open, the liquid tastes sweet but flat.

Why? In the bottling process, carbon dioxide is dissolved in soda water under high pressure. When the bottle is opened, the pressure is decreased and most of the gas rises to the surface of the liquid and escapes into the air. The tartness or acid taste desired in a cola is due to the increased amount of dissolved carbon dioxide gas in the liquid. The flat taste of the standing liquid is another indication that the dissolved carbon dioxide has escaped. Gases do not always dissolve easily in liquids, but an increase in pressure can force a gas to dissolve. The pressure inside a space suit constantly remains at about 1 atmosphere, which keeps dissolved gases in the astronaut's blood. If the space suit were punctured, pressure inside the suit would decrease and bubbles of gas would come out of the blood as did the bubbles in the cola. Not only would gas bubbles boil out of the blood, but the bubbles inside vessels would expand, causing the vessels to break. A helium-oxygen mixture is breathed by the astronauts instead of the normal air mixture of nitrogen-oxygen. Helium is used because it is less soluble in liquids. If pressure decreases suddenly inside the suit, the blood has less dissolved gas, and there are therefore fewer bubbles to escape or to expand the vessels.

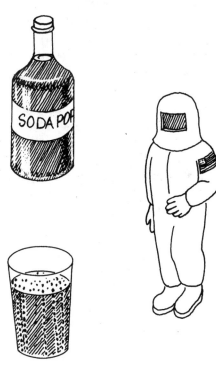

100. Sweaty

Purpose To determine what happens to water inside a closed area like a space suit.

Materials *jar with a lid*

Procedure
- *Cover the bottom of the jar with water.*
- *Close the lid.*
- *Place the jar in direct sunlight for 2 hours.*

Results Moisture collects on the inside of the jar.

Why? Heat from the Sun causes the surface water molecules inside the jar to *evaporate* (change from a liquid to a gas). When the gas hits the cool surface of the jar, it *condenses* (changes from a gas to a liquid). Human beings release salty water through the pores of their skin—perspire. The water from perspiration would evaporate and condense on different parts of the suit, as did the water inside the jar, until the entire inside of the suit was wet and uncomfortable. To prevent this, dry air enters through tubes at one part of the suit, and wet air, along with excess body heat, exits through another tube in a different part of the suit. This circulation of air provides a cool, dry environment inside the extravehicular mobility unit—the space suit.

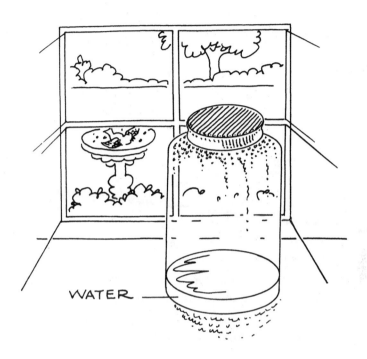

WATER

101. Taller

Purpose To simulate the effect of gravity on height.

Materials *small baby food jar*
large-mouthed jar, 1 qt. (1 liter)
2 round balloons, 9 in. (23 cm)
scissors

Procedure
- *Cut the neck from one balloon.*
- *Stretch the cut balloon over the baby food jar to cover its opening.*
- *Place the covered baby food jar inside the larger jar.*
- *Cut the tip off the rounded end of the second balloon.*
- *Stretch the balloon over the mouth of the large jar with the neck of the balloon centered over the jar's mouth.*
- *Push the surface of the stretched balloon down into the jar, allowing air from inside the jar to escape through the open neck of the balloon.*
- *Twist the balloon's neck, then pull it upward.*
- *Observe the stretched balloon over the mouth of the baby food jar.*

Results The balloon bulges upward.

Why? The jars are used to simulate the effect of gravity on the movable disc in the spinal column. Pulling the balloon upward represents a low-gravity environment, causing the rubber covering on the baby food jar to bulge upward. Pushing down on the balloon represents a high-gravity environment, and the rubber covering on the baby food jar sinks inward. In space, astronauts actually grow because of the decrease in gravity on the outside of their bodies. Gravity pulls people toward the center of the Earth, and this pull holds the separate discs in the spinal column tightly together. A reduction of gravity allows the discs to separate, resulting in instant growth. Skin, vessels, and other connecting tissue restrict the amount of disc separation. The taller space travelers experience a painful shrinking upon re-entering the Earth's gravity field when the separated discs are pulled back together.

 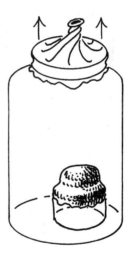

Glossary

Astrolabe—Instrument used to measure distances.

Aurora Australis—Light display in the Southern Hemisphere. Gases in the Earth's upper atmosphere glow when hit by charged particles in solar winds.

Aurora Borealis—Light display in the Northern Hemisphere. Gases in the Earth's upper atmosphere glow when hit by charged particles in solar winds.

Barycenter—Center of gravity point between the Moon-Earth system. Point at which this system moves around the Sun.

Celestial—Relating to things in the heavens.

Center of Gravity—The point at which the weight of an object is equally distributed. The object will balance at this point.

Centrifugal Force—Force created by spinning objects which pulls the object outwards.

Centripetal Force—The force pulling toward the center that keeps an object moving in a curved path.

Cephids—Variable stars that give off different amounts of light due to a change in temperature.

Cohesive Force—Attraction between like particles.

Condense—Change from gas phase to liquid phase.

Conductor—A material that transfers heat readily.

Conservation of Energy—Heat, which is a measure of the total energy of a system, remains constant. Heat lost by one substance is gained by another substance.

Constellation—A group of stars that, viewed from the Earth, form the outline of an object or figure.

Corona—Glowing gas layer around the outside of the Sun. Studied during a solar eclipse when the Moon blocks most of the Sun's light.

Deflection—To turn away.

Elliptical—A closed curve with an oval shape.

Escape Velocity—The speed necessary to break away as from the gravity field of a celestial body; for the Earth, the escape velocity is about 25,000 miles/hr (40,000 km/hr).

Evaporate—Change from liquid phase to gas phase.

Extra Vehicular Mobility Unit (EVMU)—In other words, a space suit.

Friction—Rubbing one object against another creates this force.

Galaxy—A large system of stars and other celestial bodies.

Geostationary Operational Environmental Satellite (GOES)—A satellite that has a period of rotation of 24 hours, thus appearing to remain stationary above one point on the Earth.

Geosynchronous—Remaining in the same position over the Earth.

Gravity—The attraction between two objects because of their mass. The Earth pulls everything toward its center.

Highlands—The mountainous regions on the Moon.

Inertia—Resistance to any sudden change in state, motion, or rest.

Inertia Balance—Instrument used to measure the mass of an object. Because the balance works with or without gravity, it is used to measure mass in space.

Infrared—Light waves given off by hot objects.

Insulators—Materials that help prevent temperature changes.

Light Year—Distance that light travels in one year of time, about 6 trillion miles (9.5 trillion km).

Luminous—An object that gives off its own light.

Magnetic Force Field—Area around a magnet that attracts magnetic materials.

Magnetosphere—The area around the Earth affected by its magnetic field of the Earth.

Magnitude—A measure of a star's brightness as seen from Earth.

Maria—Flat plains on the Moon.

Meteor—Meteoroids that burn in the Earth's atmosphere.

Meteorite—A meteor that reaches the Earth's surface.

Meteoroid—Large pieces of material floating in space.

Mirage—An image that is not real.

Momentum—The mass of an object times its velocity.

Nebula—A vast cloud of dust and gas in space.

Newton's Third Law of Motion—For every action, there is an equal and opposite reaction.

Opaque—Does not allow light to pass through.

Orbit—The path of an object around another body; planets moving around the Sun.

Orbiting Speed—Rate that an object moves in a curved path; the speed of planets around the Sun.

Penumbra—The lighter outer part of a shadow.

Perihelion—Point in a planet's orbit that places the planet closest to the Sun.

Period of Revolution—The time it takes one body to move around another body. Planets moving round the Sun or moons moving around a planet.

Period of Rotation—Rotation is the spinning around an axis that passes through the body.

Photometer—An instrument used to measure the brightness of a light.

Radio Waves—Energy waves produced by charged particles. Naturally emitted by the Sun and other stars. Produced by the motion of electrons in the antenna of broad-casting stations.

Reflection—The bouncing of a wave from a surface. Light and sound reflect from surfaces.

Refraction—The change of speed of light as it moves from out of one material and into another.

Resolution—The measurement of the ability to see details.

Retrograde—The backward movement of an object such as the apparent retrograde motion of Mars.

224

Retroreflector—Instrument used by NASA to measure the distance from the Earth to its Moon.

Rotation—Spinning around an axis; the Earth's movement around its imaginary axis.

Satellite—A small object that circles a larger body.

Scintillation—Scientific term used to indicate the apparent twinkling of a star.

Shadow—Area where light is blocked by an object.

Solar Eclipse—The blocking of the Sun's light by the Moon.

Solar Flare—A sudden brightness near a sunspot.

Solar Radiation—All the forms of energy given off by the Sun.

Solar Wind—A stream of charged particles from the Sun.

Spectroscope—An instrument that breaks light into its spectrum of colors.

Spiral Galaxy—A large system of stars shaped like a pin wheel.

Stellar Parallax—The difference in a star's apparent position when it is viewed from different angles.

Sunspot—A dark, cooler area on the Sun's surface. Charged particles are emitted from these areas.

Surface Tension—The tendency of the surface of a liquid to contract.

Triboluminescence—Light given off from crystals due to pressure.

Umbra—The inner darker part of a shadow.

Vacuum—A space with almost no air.

Visible Light—Waves of light that make up the colors seen in rainbows: red, orange, yellow, green, blue, and violet.

Vortex—Whirling liquid or gas with a cavity in the center toward which things are pulled. Examples are whirlpools, tornadoes, and waterspouts.

Index

227